Liners
of
Southampton
and the
Solent

By

Barry J. Eagles

For my parents, Jim and Doreen Eagles

First Published 1999   ISBN 0 946184 87 9

Front cover: A classic idyllic scene at Southampton, with the *Norway*, ex-*France*, on one of her rare visits in July 1984.

All photographs by Barry J. Eagles, unless otherwise stated.

Published By
Waterfront

A Division of Kingfisher Productions

The Dalesmade Centre, Watershed Mill, Settle,

North Yorkshire BD24 9LR

Printed by Ian Allan Printing, London

Introduction

I suppose that this book was inevitable, having been born in Southampton to a family heavily involved in shipping and the docks.

My great grandfather, James Eagles was a Dover Pilot and captained the pilot ships, *Pathfinder* and *Prudence* out of Dover harbour. His son, my grandfather was also named James Eagles and was a boilermaker at the Dover Marine packet yard of the Southern Railway. In 1936 he was transferred to the Southern Railways Steam Packet Yard in Southampton and worked on the boilers of ships such as the *Isles of Sark*, *Jersey*, *Guernsey* and later *The Falaise* and *Normannia*. My father, James Edward Eagles, completed his schooling in Dover and at the age of sixteen moved with his parents to Southampton. He also found employment in the docks for many years until his retirement in 1981. My father's maternal grandfather, John Hooper Leman also came from a seafaring background and was keeper of the East Goodwin Lightship.

My mother's family was also steeped in all things maritime. Her father, Benjamin Bartlett had served on the lavender-hulled lovelies of the Union Castle Line, and the magnificent Empress liners of Canadian Pacific in the capacity of a fireman/greaser. My mother's brother Edward, served in the catering department on many of famous ships that sailed from Southampton and my grandmother's brother, Jack Colley, was Purser onboard Cunard's beautiful *Aquitania*. My mother's family home was near Millbrook Railway Station in Southampton. It was from this house, backing on to the main railway line from Waterloo to Bournemouth that I spent most weekends. I could sit on the wall at the bottom of the garden, fortified by bottles of Tizer and sandwiches of cheese with Daddies sauce, watching the trains pass by. Maunsell's magnificent 'Lord Nelsons', 'King Arthurs', Mr Bulleid's Pacifics and some of the 'Merchant Navy' class (all thirty named after shipping companies that used Southampton Docks) would haul these trains.

Beyond the railways lines was the Western or New Docks, during school holidays I could see such ships as the *Arundel*, *Stirling*, *Athlone*, *Capetown*, *Pretoria*, *Edinburgh*, *Pendennis*, *Transvaal* and *Windsor Castles*, at 102 or 104 berth. P & O Liners such as the *Canberra*, *Oriana*, *Chusan*, *Himalaya*, *Orsorva*, *Oronsay* and *Orcades* would steam into 106 berth.

Troopships including the *Nevasa*, *Oxfordshire*, *Empire Fowey* and *Empire Orwell* would use berth 109. Ocean liner expresses and trains with Eastleigh-based and built 'Lord Nelsons', would steam by the bottom of the garden, bound for the dock sheds. Happy days indeed!

Orsova *receives attention in the No. 7 dry dock in the Western Docks in 1972.*

My mother's youngest brother, my Uncle and great friend Ernie, still lives in that house, but alas motorised carriages now run along the electrified lines. A road runs between the railway lines and docks, but the floating blocks of flats that now pass as cruise ships, are all that can be seen nowadays.

I started my working life in various jobs before I became employed by the Mercantile Marine Office and Union Castle, signing on and off ship's crews. I then spent twenty years working in sales and marketing for a well-known American company before taking early retirement and escaping from the rat race. I now write scripts, provide archive cine footage for railway and shipping videos as well as holding an extensive colour slide library of steam. I have the honour of being the publicity officer and one of the pursers of the S S *Shieldhall*, Europe's largest fully operational, preserved passenger and cargo steamship.

The Port of Southampton has been the gateway to the world for most of this century, with its very beginnings going way back to 1838. But it was in

Thanks also to Ron Hancock, of Associated British Ports for his help with dock passes and information; my great friend Captain Alistair Cant for his inspiration and company over many a wee dram. Other friends such as Max Coaker, operations manager of Southampton Container berth, Bill Windebank, Bert Moody, Ernie Bartlett, Andy Crespin, Pam and David Bates, and my publisher Roger Hardingham, for pinning me down to produce this book. There have been many other friends who have been of help and I must not forget my long-suffering wife Carol and my children James and Charlotte, who have come to understand my interests.

Technical details

Most of the slides have been taken on various Kodachrome films over the years. This film seems to survive the ravages of time. The camera I used until 1979 was a Pentax SV 35-mm single lens reflex with a F1.4 super Takumar lens. I now use a Nikon FE and a Nikon F90X 35-mm single lens reflex camera with several different Nikon lenses.

Barry James Eagles, Southampton

the early part of the 20th century that the liners started to arrive from Liverpool and Southampton hasn't looked back since. The heydays were undoubtedly in the 1930s and following the Second World War, in the 1950s. So shake those sea legs, cast off the shorelines and come with me to view the ships in the Docks and along Southampton water.

As well as my parents, I must thank the skippers of the Red Funnel tugs, *Thornness* and *Calshot,* Captain George Howard and the late Captain Steve Pascoe who both looked after me very well indeed. I have learnt a la great deal about the sea fromthem as well as acquiring some of my best 'underway' shots from their commands as they attended to the arrivals and departures of these great liners.

*Top left: The mantle for looking after elderly, although still useful liners, has now passed to Premier Cruiselines, this line really looks after its old ladies. All their ships are well maintained and kept immaculate, all having been brought up to the latest stringent Safety and Life at Sea regulations (SOLAS). Their fleet consists of the **Rembrandt** seen on a clear day at Southampton in October 1998.*
*Lower right: The elderly **Queen Frederika** is seen in King George V dry dock at Southampton in October 1970. This 1926-built liner was withdrawn the following year.*

R M S Queen Elizabeth

The old adage that 'if it looks right, it is right', certainly applied to the mighty *Queen Elizabeth* of the Cunard Line! Samuel Cunard founded the Cunard line in 1840. Many fine ships were built for them, the *Queen Elizabeth* being the largest of all, constructed by John Brown on the Clyde and launched on 27th September 1938 by her sponsor Queen Elizabeth, now the Queen Mother. Her maiden voyage to New York was scheduled for the 24th April 1940 but due to the intervention of the Second World War, this became impossible. Her true maiden voyage began from Southampton on 16th October 1946 sailing to New York and for the next twenty-two years she worked the Atlantic Bridge with her running companion the *Queen Mary*. She left her homeport of Southampton for the very last time on 29th November 1968 bound for Port Everglades in the USA. After a stay of several years, the C Y Shipping group of Hong Kong bought her and converted her into a floating university named the *Seawise University*. On the 9th January 1972 she caught fire in Hong Kong harbour and became a total loss. Photograph, August 1965, collection of Barry J. Eagles. **Technical Details.-** The *Queen Elizabeth* was powered by Parson's geared turbines, driving quadruple screws developing 200,000-shaft horsepower, giving a maximum speed of 32 knots. Her length was 1029 feet and a gross registered tonnage of 83,673. She was designed to carry 2283 passengers in three classes with a crew of 1,296.

4

R M S Queen Mary   Everyone's favourite ship was built by John Brown on the Clyde. Her launching, delayed by a World of economic depression, was performed by Queen Mary, the consort of King George V on 26th September 1934. She was handed over to the now Cunard White Star Line on 11th May 1936. On 27th May 1936, dressed overall, she left Southampton for Cherbourg and New York on her maiden voyage. Her war service as a troopship paralleled the *Queen Elizabeth* although she had the misfortune to collide with, and sank, the cruiser *H M S Curacoa* with the loss of 329 crew members. She held the Blue Riband of the Atlantic for some fourteen years until she was usurped by the *S S United States* in 1952. She too became a victim of air travel and was sold to the City of Long Beach, California as a hotel and convention centre. The *Queen Mary* had a tremendous send off from Southampton, where she left for the last time on 31st October 1967, arriving at Long Beach on 9th December 1967. She is seen departing Southampton in July 1962, collection of Barry J. Eagles.
Technical Details - Powered by Parson's geared turbines, driving quadruple screws, developing 200,000-shaft horsepower, giving a maximum speed of 32 knots. Her length was 1,019 feet and gross registered tonnage of 80,774. She carried 2,139 passengers in three classes and a crew of 1,101.

Mauretania Named after the greatly lamented four-funnelled Cunarder, the second *Mauretania* was built at the Birkenhead shipyard of Cammell Laird. Lady Bates, the wife of the Cunard chairman, launched her on the 28th July 1938. At the time of her launch she was the largest ship ever to have been constructed in an English shipyard. Her maiden voyage was from Liverpool to New York, on which she sailed on 17th June 1939. The Second World War soon interrupted her sailings and she was sent to Sydney, Australia for conversion to a troop transport. It was not until the 26th April 1947 that she made her first post-war crossing from Liverpool to New York. She was used for full time cruising from 1962 and was painted in Cunard's pleasing pale green livery. *Mauretania* was only used in this capacity for three years and on the 23rd November 1965 she arrived at T W Wards, shipbreaking yard at Inverkeithing. Collection of Barry J. Eagles. **Technical Details -** Powered by Parson's geared turbines, driving twin screws, producing 42,000-shaft horsepower, giving a maximum speed of 23 knots. Her length was 772 feet and her gross registered tonnage was 35,738. She carried when built 1,360 passengers in three classes and a crew of 780.

Caronia Cunard's beautiful 'Green Goddess' - *Caronia*, was launched at the Clydeside yard of John Brown by the then, Princess Elizabeth, on the 30th October 1947. She was painted in Cunard's green cruising livery for the whole of her service with them. Her maiden voyage from Southampton to New York took place on the 4th January 1949. She was renowned for her annual around the world cruises and carried so many millionaires that she became known as the millionaire's yacht. It was said that her single funnel was the largest on any British ship. With the advent of more fuel economic ships, Cunard reluctantly withdrew her. After several months laid up in Southampton, *Caronia* was sold to an American-backed Panamanian company for the sum of £1,250,000. After two cruises full of problems she was laid up in New York for five years. Eventually she was sold for scrapping and on her way to a Taiwanese yard, whilst under tow on the 12th August 1974, she hit the breakwater at Apra and broke into three parts. A dramatic ending for a beautiful ship. Photographed in May 1966, collection of Barry J. Eagles. **Technical Details** - Powered by geared turbine, driving twin screws, developing 35,000-shaft horsepower, and giving a top speed of 22 knots. Her length was 715 feet and a gross registered tonnage of 34,183. As built she carried 932 passengers in two classes and a crew of 600.

Saxonia The lead ship of the quartet of Cunarders, known officially as the Saxonia class and unofficially as the 600 footers, was built by John Brown's shipyard on the Clyde. Lady Churchill, wife of Sir Winston Churchill, launched *Saxonia* on the 17th February 1954. Her maiden voyage was from Liverpool to Montreal and commenced on the 2nd September 1954. During 1962 she was returned to her builders and refitted for full time cruising. Her draught tonnage was increased and after being repainted in Cunard's cruising green she was renamed *Carmania*. Withdrawn by Cunard in October 1971, she was laid up in Southampton and the River Fal for two years before being sold to the Soviet State Black Sea Shipping Company of Odessa, and renamed *Leonid Sobinov* (see page 44). This elegant stern view was taken at Ocean Dock in September 1961, from the collection of Barry J. Eagles. **Technical Details** - Powered by geared steam turbines, driving twin screws, developing 24,500-shaft horsepower, giving a maximum speed of 22 knots. Her length is 608 feet and a gross registered tonnage of 21,637. As built she carried 929 passengers in two classes with a crew of 461.

Carmania (formerly the *Saxonia* - see opposite page) & *Franconia*. *Carmania* originally known as the *Saxonia*, and *Franconia* had very similar careers, they were both built by John Brown on the Clyde. *Franconia* was built as the *Ivernia* and was launched by Mrs C D Howe, the wife of the then Canadian minister of trade. Her maiden voyage from Liverpool to Montreal commenced on the 27th July 1955. She was returned to her builders in October 1962 and refitted for cruising. This increased her gross registered tonnage to 22,637. Repainted in Cunard's cruising green, she was renamed *Franconia*. Four years later she was repainted white and withdrawn from Cunard's service in 1971. She was laid up alongside her sister, *Franconia* at 101 Berth in Southampton (photographed above in July 1972) and then in the River Fal. In August 1973 she was sold to the Russians and renamed *Fedor Shalyapin*.

Technical Details - Powered by geared steam turbines driving twin screws, developing 24,500-shaft horsepower, giving a maximum speed of 22 knots. Her length is 608 feet and a gross registered tonnage of 21,717. As built she carried 943 passengers in two classes with a crew of 461.

Queen Elizabeth II (QE2)

Cunard's favourite builder, John Brown's Shipyard, built the last transatlantic Cunarder. Her Majesty the Queen launched her on the 20th September 1967. On the 23rd December 1968 the *QE2* left Greenock on her acceptance cruise to the Canary Islands. On Christmas Eve trouble was experienced with both her turbines and Cunard refused to accept delivery from her builders. She limped into Southampton on the 2nd January 1969. It was four months later that she was finally accepted by Cunard and left Southampton for New York on the 2nd May. For the next thirteen years she voyaged across the Atlantic. Her moment of glory came on the 4th May 1982 when she sailed from Southampton with troops bound for South Georgia in the South Atlantic. In 1986 Cunard took the decision to replace the *QE2's* steam turbines and put in nine Burmeister and Wain MAN diesel electric engines. Lloyd Werfte of Bremerhaven completed this task in six months and she returned to service with the same shaft horsepower and speed as before. At the end of the 20th Century she is as popular as ever and there is even talk of a running companion being built by Cunard's new owners, the Carnival Cruise Company. She is seen at Southampton in May 1971 in her original form. **Technical Details** - As built she was powered by geared steam turbines driving twin screws, developing 110,000-shaft horsepower, giving a maximum speed of 28.5 knots. Her length is 963 feet and a gross registered tonnage of 65,863. She carried 2005 passengers in two classes but only 1400 in one class when cruising with a crew of 906.

R M S Arundel Castle Every Thursday at 4 o'clock, a Union Castle liner would leave Southampton bound for South Africa. Harland and Wolff of Belfast originally built the *Arundel Castle* as a four-funnelled ship. She had been laid down in 1915 and was to have been called the *Amroth Castle* but was not launched until the 11th September 1919 being the first Union Castle liner to be powered by steam turbines. The *Arundel Castle*'s maiden voyage from Southampton to Capetown commenced on the 22nd April 1921. In 1937 she was refitted and was re-engined and lengthened, losing two of her funnels in the process. She was used as a troopship during the Second World War and it was not until September 1950 that she was returned to her owners. The *Arundel Castle* departed for her final destination on the 30th December 1958. In her career of 37 ½ years she had steamed a total of 3,475,565 miles. German aircraft sank her sister ship, the *Windsor Castle* on the 23rd March 1943. She is seen at 103 Berth just six months before withdrawal, from the collection of Barry J. Eagles. **Technical Details** - Powered by geared steam turbines driving twin screws, developing 15,000-shaft horsepower, giving a maximum speed of 18 knots. After her 1937 refit her speed was increased to 20 knots. Her length was 686 feet with a gross registered tonnage of 19,118. She carried 580 passengers in three classes.

Left: **R M M V Stirling Castle**   *Stirling Castle* and her sister the *Athlone Castle* were both built by Harland and Wolff of Belfast. *Stirling Castle* was launched on the 15th July 1935 by Mrs Robertson Gibb, the wife of the company chairman. Her maiden voyage from Southampton to Capetown commenced on the 7th February 1936. Later that year she broke the record for the fastest time to the Cape, which had been held by the Union Line's *Scott* for forty-three years. The *Stirling Castle* was released from war duties in 1946 and was overhauled by Harland and Wolff and returned to the mail service in 1947. Her last arrival at Southampton from the Cape was on the 30th November 1965.   Her sister, the *Athlone Castle*, had already been withdrawn and had arrived at Kaohsiung, Taiwan for scrapping on the 13th September 1965. Photographed in September 1964, from the collection of Barry J. Eagles.
Technical Details - Powered by two ten-cylinder Burmeister and Wain oil engines driving twin screws, developing 24,000-brake horsepower, giving a maximum speed of 20 knots. Her length was 725 feet with a gross registered tonnage of 25,550. As built she carried 789 passengers in two classes.

Above: **R M S Edinburgh Castle**   The *Edinburgh Castle* and the *Pretoria Castle* were sister ships, built by Harland and Wolff of Belfast; *Edinburgh Castle* being launched on 16th October 1947. These two ships reverted Union Castle liners back to steam turbine propulsion. The *Edinburgh Castle* was the first ship to use the new Union Castle terminal at 102 berth in Southampton Docks on the 10th February 1956. In 1962 she was refitted; the only outward sign was the re-arranging and the shortening of her masts. She commenced her last round trip from Southampton on the 5th March 1976. On the 3rd June 1976 she arrived at Kaohsiung, Taiwan where she was broken up. Her sister ship, the *Pretoria Castle* was renamed the *S A Oranje* (see page 43).
Technical Details - Powered by geared steam turbines driving twin screws, developing 35,000-shaft horsepower, giving a maximum speed of 22 knots. Her length was 747 feet with a gross registered tonnage of 28,705. She carried 755 passengers in two classes with a crew of 400.

R M S Pendennis Castle
The *Pendennis Castle* was the first Union Castle liner to be fitted with stabilisers. She was built by Harland and Wolff of Belfast and was due to be launched on the 10th December 1957 by the dowager Lady Rotherwick. However, she did not take to the water until the 24th December due to an industrial dispute. This had serious repercussions for Harland and Wolff because the board of British and Commonwealth, the owners of the Union Castle vowed never to have another ship built by them. Her maiden voyage commenced on New Year's Day 1959 from Southampton to the Cape. Her last arrival at Southampton was on the 14th June 1976 after which she was sold to the Ocean Queen Navigation Corporation of Panama and renamed *Ocean Queen*. At the end of 1977 she was sold again and renamed at first *Sinbad*, and later *Sinbad 1*. Unfortunately she never carried a single passenger for her new owners and after arrival at Kaohsiung in April 1980, she was broken up. Photographed July 1975.

Technical Details - Powered by Parson's geared turbines driving twin screws, developing 46,000-shaft horsepower, giving a maximum speed of 22.5 knots. Her length was 763 feet with a gross registered tonnage of 28,582. She carried 670 passengers in two classes.

RMS Windsor Castle   This ship was the largest ever built for the Union Castle Line. She was built by Cammell Laird of Birkenhead and was launched on the 23rd June 1959 by Queen Elizabeth, the Queen Mother. The *Windsor Castle*'s maiden voyage was from Southampton to Capetown on the 18th August 1960. For the next 17 years she plied faithfully to and from South Africa one hundred and twenty four times. On the 6th September 1977 she had a splendid farewell from Capetown and arrived at Southampton thirteen days later. She was sold to John S Latsis of Athens and renamed the *Margarita L*. On the 3rd October 1977 she left for Piraeus for conversion into a luxury-floating hotel in Jeddah, Saudi Arabia. She is currently laid up in Eleusis Bay near Athens. Photographed May 1976. **Technical Details** - Powered by Parson's geared turbines driving twin screws, producing 49,000-shaft horsepower, and giving a maximum speed of 23 knots. Her length is 783 feet with a gross registered tonnage of 37,640. She carried 782 passengers in two classes with a crew of 475.

Reina del Mar   Ordered for the Pacific Steam Navigation Company's Service from Liverpool to South America. She was built by Harland and Wolff of Belfast and was launched on the 7th June 1955. Her maiden voyage from Liverpool to Valparaiso commenced on the 3rd May 1956. On 10th March 1964 she was sent to Harland and Wolff to be converted to a full time cruise ship, managed by the Union Castle Line. Her owners, Pacific Steam Navigation sold the *Reina del Mar* to Union Castle in September 1973. This ownership did not last long as on the 30th July 1975 she arrived at Kaohsiung to be broken up by the Tung Cheng Steel Manufacturing Company. Photographed May 1975. **Technical Details -** Powered by Parson's geared turbines driving twin screws, developing 17,000-shaft horsepower, giving a maximum speed of 18 knots. Her length was 601 feet with a gross registered tonnage of 20,234. As built she carried 766 passengers in three classes with a crew of 327. After refitting as a cruise ship she carried 1,047 passengers in one class.

Oronsay The *Oronsay* was built by Vickers Armstrong Ltd of Barrow and was launched on the 30th June 1950. Whilst fitting out she accidentally caught fire which took three days to bring under control. This caused her maiden voyage from Tilbury to Sidney to be delayed by two months. In April 1964 *Oronsay* was the first Orient liner to be transferred to P & O ownership. She was painted in P & O's white livery instead of her distinctive Orient corn-colour. Towards the end of her career *Oronsay* was cruising full time. Many cruises originated from Australia and she was very popular in that part of the World. Her last cruise from Southampton commenced on the 22nd July 1975.   During her 25-year career she completed 64 line voyages and 37 cruises. Photographed in morning sunlight in August 1975. **Technical Details** - Powered by Parson's geared turbines driving twin screws, developing 42,500-shaft horsepower, giving a maximum speed of 26 knots. Her length was 708 feet with a gross registered tonnage of 27,632. As built she carried 1501 passengers in two classes. Later when cruising she carried 1,400 tourist class passengers with a crew of 622.

Orsova   The Second World War had been exceptionally bad for the Orient Line, as it had lost half its fleet of eight ships. When the conflict ended they ordered three new ships, the *Orcades,* the *Oronsay* (see page17) and the last of the trio, *Orsova.* Like her two sisters *Orsova* was built by Vickers Armstrong at Barrow and was launched on the 14th May 1953. She was built slightly larger than her two sisters and sailed on her maiden voyage from Tilbury to Australia on the 17th March 1954. In 1960 P & O merged with Orient to form a new Company P & O Orient Lines. By 1964 the *Orsova* was re-painted into P & O white. In 1973 it was announced that P & O's *Canberra* (see page25) would be withdrawn and that *Orsova* would take over her cruising programme. In August 1973 the position was reversed; *Orsova's* final months were spent cruising from Southampton, her final cruise commencing on 25th November 1973. She departed from Southampton for the last time on the 14th December 1973 and met her end at the Nan Feng Steel Enterprise Company at Kaohsiung. Photographed at 106 Berth in August 1973. **Technical Details** - Powered by Parson's geared turbines driving twin screws, developing 42,500-shaft horsepower, giving a maximum speed of 26 knots. Her length was 723 feet with a gross registered tonnage of 28,790. She carried 1,494 passengers in two classes with a crew of 620.

Oriana   This was the last ship to be built for the Orient Line and by far the largest. She was built by Orient Line's favoured builders Vickers Armstrong of Barrow in Furness. Although she had a fairly traditional hull, her superstructure was quite revolutionary. Her homeport was Southampton and she sailed on her maiden voyage to Australia from there on the 3rd December 1960. The *Oriana* soon gained the 'Golden Cockerel' as the fastest ship from England to Australia. Her corn-coloured hull was painted in P & O's white in early 1965. On the 11th August 1970 her boiler room caught fire. *Oriana* would have been lost if it had not been for the prompt attention of the fireboats. 1981 was to be her final UK cruising season and she departed from Southampton for the last time on the 12th November 1981. The next four and a half years saw *Oriana* cruise out of Sydney, Australia. She completed her last cruise on the 27th March 1986 and two months later she was towed to Beppu on the Southern Island of Kyushu in Japan for use as a floating hotel. She is currently serving the same purpose in China.   **Technical Details** - Powered by Parson's geared turbines driving twin screws, developing 80,000-shaft horsepower, giving a maximum speed of 30.5 knots. Her length was 804 feet with a gross registered tonnage of 41,915. She carried 2,136 passengers in two classes or 1,700 in one class only, with a crew of 903.

Strathmore   The Peninsular and Steam Ship Company, more commonly known as P & O, embarked on a series of five liners in the 1930s, *Strathmore* was the third. She was built by Vickers Armstrong of Barrow and was launched by the former Duchess of York, now the Queen Mother, on the 4th April 1935. Her maiden voyage was a two-week cruise to the Atlantic Isles, Dakar, Cadiz and Lisbon, and departed from Tilbury on the 27th of September 1935. *Strathmore* resumed her Australian voyages on the 27th October 1949 after a post-war refit. In 1961 she was converted to a one-class ship and then sold to John S Latsis for further use as a hotel and pilgrim ship in October 1963. She was at first renamed *Marianna Latsi* and three years later it was changed to *Henrietta Latsi*. In June 1969 she was sold to Italian shipbreakers for demolition at La Spezia. Photographed proudly displaying the Blue Ensign in April 1963, from the collection of Barry J Eagles.   **Technical Details** - Powered by Parson's geared turbines driving twin screws, developing 28,000-shaft horsepower, giving a maximum speed of 22 knots. Her length was 665 feet with a gross registered tonnage of 23,428. As built she carried 1,100 passengers in two classes with a crew of 515.

Stratheden *Stratheden* was the fourth of the Straths and had the same birthplace as her sisters, Vickers Armstrong of Barrow. Her maiden voyage to Brisbane commenced on the 24th December 1937 and in March 1940 like her sisters, she was requisitioned as a troop ship. She was to carry 149,697 personnel and steamed 468,000 miles during her war service. On the 13th March 1955 she answered a distress call from the Greek trawler, *Jason* which was sinking off Southern Italy. A lifeboat was launched but was capsized by the heavy seas, causing eight of her crew to lose their lives. Only four of the trawler's crew of 17 were rescued. She was sold, and handed over to John S Latsis Company in Piraeus on the 18th February 1964, being renamed *Henrietta Latsi*. She worked in conjunction with her sister, the *Marianna Latsi*, carrying pilgrims to Jeddah, the port for Mecca in Saudi Arabia. *Stratheden's* end came in June 1969 when she was sold to be broken up at La Spezia in Italy. Photographed in July 1958, from the collection of Barry J. Eagles.

Technical Details - Powered by Parson's geared turbines driving twin screws, developing 28,000-shaft horsepower, giving a maximum speed of 22 knots. Her length was 664 feet with a gross registered tonnage of 23,722. As built she carried 1,011 passengers in two classes and latterly 1,200 passengers in one class with a crew of 563.

Left: **Chusan** *Chusan* took her name from the Chusan Archipelago off Shanghai. She was the second ship of P & O's post war re-building programme and was built by Vickers Armstrong of Barrow. She cost £3,250,000 to build and she was the most sophisticated and luxurious of the ships built for P & O's Far Eastern service. *Chusan* was the first ship to be fitted with Denny-Brown stabilisers and during her 1959/60 refit had her air-conditioning extended throughout the whole ship. She made P & O's last scheduled passenger call at Bombay on the 8th February 1970. In December 1972 her withdrawal was announced and on the 12th May 1973 she left Southampton for the last time bound for Kaohsuing, Taiwan where she was broken up. Photographed in bright sunshine in April 1973. **Technical Details** - Powered by Parson's double reduction geared turbines driving twin screws, developing 42,500-shaft horsepower, giving a maximum speed of 22 knots. Her length was 673 feet with a gross registered tonnage on 24,215. As built she carried 1,026 passengers in two classes with a crew of 572.

Above: **Himalaya** The P & O Shipping Group lost 182 vessels during the Second World War. The re-building of the passenger fleet commenced in January 1946 with the ordering of the *Himalaya* from Vickers Armstrong of Barrow. On the 27th August 1956 *Himalaya* experienced an explosion in the refrigeration plant which unfortunately caused the death of five crewmembers. In 1963 she was refitted as a one-class ship with a capacity for 1,416 passengers. For the next 11 years she sailed out of Southampton and then Sydney. It was from that port on the 19th October 1974 that she sailed to the breakers yard at Kaohsiung, Taiwan. Photographed in May 1974. **Technical Details** - Powered by Parson's double reduction geared turbines driving twin screws, developing 42,500-shaft horsepower, giving a maximum speed of 22 knots. Her length was 709 feet with a gross registered tonnage of 27,955. As built she carried 1,159 passengers in two classes with a crew of 631.

Arcadia   The *Arcadia* was a beautifully proportioned ship and was a great success for P & O as an ocean liner and cruise ship. She was built by John Brown on the Clyde and on the 14th May 1953 was launched by Mrs D E Anderson, the wife of P & O's deputy chairman. *Arcadia* sailed on her maiden voyage from Tilbury to Sydney on the 22nd February 1954 and gained a reputation for efficiency and comfort. On the 1st April 1959 *Arcadia* was sent to Harland and Wolff in Belfast for refitting and full air-conditioning. By 1968 she was cruising mainly in the Pacific and was given another refit in early 1975, this time by Vosper Thorneycroft in Southampton. On the 1st September 1978 P & O announced that the *Sea Princess* (see page26) would replace her. During her 25 years she had steamed 2,650,000 miles and had carried 430,000 passengers. Photographed in May 1976.
Technical Details - Powered by Parson's geared turbines driving twin screws, developing 42,500-shaft horsepower, giving a maximum speed of 25 knots. Her length was 721 feet with a gross registered tonnage of 29,734. She carried 1,410 passengers in two classes with a crew of 710.

Canberra The *Canberra* was known affectionately as 'the great white whale', due to her exploits in the Falklands War. She was built by Harland and Wolff of Belfast and Dame Pattie Menzies, the wife of the Australian Prime Minister, launched her on the 16th March 1960. The writing was on the wall by late 1973 for line voyages to Australia, and early in 1974 *Canberra* was converted into a one-class ship for permanent cruising. On the 7th April 1982 she was back in Southampton for conversion into a troop ship. With a full compliment of troops she left Southampton on the 9th April 1982 bound for the South Atlantic. By the 20th May she was anchored in San Carlos Water, the next day she disembarked her troops and then sailed to rendezvous with the *QE2* in South Georgia. *Canberra* arrived back to a tumultuous reception at Southampton on the 11th July 1982. On the 30th September 1997, *Canberra* sailed into Southampton for the very last time, to another rousing reception. A few weeks later she sailed for Gadani Beach, Pakistan where she was broken up.
Technical Details - Powered by Turbo Electric British Thompson Houston engines, driving twin screws, developing 88,000-shaft horsepower, giving a maximum speed of 29 knots. Her length was 820 feet with a gross registered tonnage of 45,270. As built she carried 2,198 passengers in two classes with a crew of 900.

Sea Princess   In June 1978, P & O announced that they had bought the Swedish/American Liner, *Kunsgholm* (see page41) to replace the *Arcadia* (see page 24). (*Kungsholm* had been built by John Brown on the Clyde, and launched on the 14th April 1965.) P & O sent her to the Bremer Vulkan yard at Bremen for refitting. The forward funnel was removed and the remaining one was heightened. For the next few years she cruised out of Australia until replaced by the *Oriana* (see page 28). She arrived back at Southampton on the 21st April 1982 for a three-week refit by Vosper Thorneycroft. This was only thirteen days after the *Canberra* (see page25) had sailed for the Falklands. It was thought that *Sea Princess* would join her as a troopship but this was not to be, and she sailed on a Mediterranean cruise on the 14th May 1982. By 1985 she was cruising to new areas, on the 9th March 1985 she visited Shanghai for the first time. On the 27th April 1995 she was renamed the *Victoria*, and keeps alive the traditional cruising spirit of P & O. Photographed in January 1979.

Technical Details - Powered by Gotaverken direct drive diesel engines driving twin screws, developing 25,200-brake horsepower, giving a maximum speed of 23 knots. Her length is 660 feet with a gross registered tonnage of 27,670. She carries 750 passengers in one class with a crew of 402.

Island Princess   The motor ship *Island Princess* was built for Norwegian Cruise Ships of Oslo as the *Island Venture*. She was built by Rheinstahl Nordsee Werke of Emden and was launched on the 6th March 1971. After completion of trials she was named *Island Venture* at Oslo, on the 14th December 1971. As built she carried 767 passengers and a crew of 317. On the 4th January 1972 she started cruising from New York to Hamilton under the ownership of Flagship Cruises Ltd of New York. In September that year *Island Venture* came under the sole ownership of Fearnley and Eger of Oslo and was renamed *Island Princess*. She continued cruising from United States ports and in November 1972 she was chartered to Princess Cruises, a company which is now owned by P&O. *Island Princess* has recently made a few summer cruises from Southampton. Princess Cruises have recently ordered several large cruise ships, and the days of P & O ownership of *Island Princess* and her sister must be surely numbered. Photographed in July 1976.

Technical Details - Powered by four, ten-cylindered, geared Fiat diesels driving twin screws, developing 18,000-brake horsepower, giving a maximum speed of 21.5 knots. Her length is 553 feet with a gross registered tonnage of 19,907. She carries 600 passengers in one class.

Oriana   The second ship named *Oriana* built for the Peninsular and Oriental Shipping Company at the Meyer Werft shipyard in Germany. She arrived in Southampton for the first time on the 3rd April 1995 with Her Majesty the Queen naming the liner in the port on the 6th April 1995. P & O claimed her to be the fastest cruise ship built for 25 years and she departed Southampton on her maiden cruise on the 9th April 1995 to the Canary Islands, Morocco and Lisbon. *Oriana* is the first big ship to be built specifically for the British Cruise market and did not have to serve the traditional P & O role of being built primarily for line voyages. She is now in her fourth year of service and spends the winter cruising around the World and returns to Southampton in April, for her UK - based cruising season. She has become a very popular ship and P&O have announced that a larger version of her is currently being built and will be named the *Aurora*. Photographed in July 1996. **Technical Details** - Powered by four Mann diesels driving twin screws, giving a service speed of 24 knots. Her length is 850 feet with a gross registered tonnage of 67,000. She carries 1,760 passengers in one class with a crew of 760.

SS Uganda   The *Uganda* was a very popular ship, made famous by the Falklands War in which she served as a hospital ship. Her affectionate nickname during this conflict was 'the Mother Hen'. She was built for the British India Line by Barclay Curle & Company of Glasgow and she was originally intended to be named *Karatina*. For the next fifteen years she sailed on the East-African run with her sister *Kenya*. The service ended in 1967 and was *Kenya* scrapped but *Uganda* was sent to the Howaldte Werke of Hamburg where she rebuilt as a schools' cruise ship. She arrived there on the 5th April 1967 and on the 27th February 1968 she made her first cruise in her new role. She was transferred to P & O ownership on the 5th December 1972 but continued in this role until the 13th April 1982 when she was requisitioned as a hospital ship. At the conclusion of this charter, *Uganda* was laid up in the River Fal for a year. On the 29th April 1986 *Uganda* left her lay-up berth and was towed to breakers in Taiwan. However, she was caught by typhoon 'Wayne' near Kaohsiun and was driven ashore where she collapsed on her side and was subsequently broken up. Photographed in April 1976.
Technical Details - Powered by geared turbines, driving twin screws, developing 12,300-shaft horsepower, giving a maximum speed of 19.5 knots. Her length was 539 feet with a gross registered tonnage of 16,907. She carried 306 cabin passengers and 920 children.

SS Nevasa *Nevasa* was built as a troop transport for the British India Line and was often called the 'centenary' ship as she was delivered in the centenary year of that company. She was built by Barclay Curle and Company of Glasgow and was launched by Mrs J A Boyd-Carpenter, the wife of the then Minister of Transport on the 30th November 1955. She was painted in the distinctive troop ship livery, of white hull with a broad blue band and a yellow funnel. In 1962 the government decided that all future troop transporting would be continued by air and consequently *Nevasa's* contract was ended. After her last trooping voyage in September 1962, she arrived in the River Fal for laying up. She remained there for two years, until she was sent to the Falmouth yard of Silley Cox and Company Ltd for refitting. She emerged as an educational cruise ship and on the 28th October 1965 she made her first cruise in her new capacity from Southampton. During 1972 British India Ships were transferred to P&O ownership. Being the largest of all the educational cruise ships, was not necessarily to her advantage as there were many ports that she was unable to get into because of her draught. She was sold on the 2nd April 1975 to the Nan Feng Steel Enterprise Company of Kaohsiung, Taiwan for demolition, a premature end to a fine ship. Photographed in September 1971.

Technical Details - Powered by Parson's geared turbines, driving twin screws, developing 20,280-shaft horsepower, giving a maximum speed of 21 knots. Her length was 609 feet with a gross registered tonnage of 20,527. She carried 308 cabin passengers and 1090 children.

Aureol   *Aureol* was the last passenger ship built for the Elder Dempster Line of Liverpool. A beautiful ship, built on the lines of a large, private motor yacht; she commenced her maiden voyage from Liverpool to Lagos on the 12th October 1951. For the next 21 years, she plied between Liverpool and Lagos. In 1972 Elder Dempster sent the *Aureol* to sail out of Southampton, her first voyage from this port commencing on the 26th April. By the mid 1970s the winds of change were sweeping through Africa and this coupled with air travel was making in roads into the number of passengers wishing to travel by sea. It therefore came as no surprise when Elder Dempster announced that the *Aureol* would be withdrawn. She was refitted at Piraeus as an accommodation ship and renamed the *Marianna VI* and moored at Jeddah in Saudi Arabia until 1979. *Marianna VI* arrived at the Gulf of Eleusis near Piraeus on the 8th December 1989 and at the present time she is still laid up there. Photographed in June 1974.

Technical Details - Powered by Doxford diesels, driving twin screws, developing 10,800 brake horsepower, giving a maximum speed of 16 knots. Her length is 537 feet with a gross registered tonnage of 14,083. As built she carried 353 passengers in two classes with a crew of 145.

R M S Andes   *Andes* was built as the centenary ship of the Royal Mail Lines for their South American service. She was still fitting out when the Second World War was declared and was completed as a troop transport. In this capacity she made her first voyage on the 9th December 1939 to Halifax, returning fully loaded with Canadian troops. In May 1945 she carried the exiled Norwegian government back to Oslo where she had a tremendous reception. Finally released from war service in 1947, she was sent back to her builders to be refitted as a passenger ship. *Andes* was the largest and fastest liner on the South American run, and made her first voyage from London to La Plato on the 22nd January 1948. She was rebuilt as a cruise liner in 1960 in Holland and in the course of this rebuild her hull was painted white. She cruised on for another 11 years but unfortunately her age and rising operating costs were working against her and Royal Mail reluctantly decided to withdraw her. On the 7th May 1971 she arrived in Ghent to be broken up by the Van Heyghen Freres. Photograph from the collection of Barry J. Eagles.   **Technical Details** - Powered by geared turbines, driving twin screws, developing 30,000-shaft horsepower, giving a maximum speed of 21 knots. Her length was 669 feet with a gross registered tonnage of 25,895. When rebuilt for cruising she carried 480 passengers in one class.

Southern Cross The *Southern Cross* was ahead of her time, she was the first major passenger liner with engines aft. She was built by Harland & Wolff of Belfast for Shaw Savill and Albion and was launched on the 17th August 1954 by Her Majesty, the Queen. She was mainly used on the £10 assisted passage emigration scheme to Australia. *Southern Cross*'s running companion on this service was at first the *Dominion Monarch*. Her itinerary was for four voyages a year, two westbound and two eastbound. After the assisted passage scheme came to an end in the late 1960s, *Southern Cross* made a few cruises in 1971 but was withdrawn in early 1972. She was sold for £500,000 to the Companhia de Vapores of Panama and renamed *Calypso* (see page57) and registered in Ithaca. She had served Shaw Savill and Albion for nearly 20 years, but is still to be in service 26 years later with no sign of being withdrawn. Photographed in June 1967, from the collection of Barry J. Eagles. **Technical Details** - Powered by geared turbines, driving twin screws, developing 20,000-shaft horsepower, giving a maximum speed of 21 knots. Her length is 604 feet with a gross registered tonnage of 20,204. She carried 1,160 tourist class passengers.

Northern Star   Built as the running companion to the *Southern Cross*, *Northern Star* only had a short life of 12 years after being launched by Queen Elizabeth the Queen Mother on the 27th June 1961 at Vickers Armstrong. She left on her maiden voyage from Southampton on the 10th July 1962 with a full compliment of passengers. *Northern Star* would depart from Southampton every three months and would take either the eastbound route, via Capetown or the westbound route via Panama to Australia and New Zealand. On her maiden voyage *Northern Star* experienced problems with her high pressure turbines, but was able to continue her voyage on her low pressure ones. She made Sydney but the turbines failed again when she departed from Tahiti, causing her to arrive in Southampton nine days late. In March 1966 *Northern Star*'s funnel colour of the traditional Shaw Savill buff, was changed to dark Aberdeen green, with a large yellow star on either side. After the withdrawal of the *Southern Cross*, a running companion had been sought for her and Shaw Savill bought the Canadian Pacific liner, *Empress of England* and renamed her *Ocean Monarch* (see opposite page). Only three years after the purchase of this ship, Shaw Savill decided to withdraw *Northern Star*.   She completed her last cruise from Southampton on the 1st November 1974 and one month later she arrived at the Li Chong Steel and Iron Works where she was broken up. Photographed in June 1975.

Technical Details - Powered by Parson's geared turbines, driving twin screws, developing 22,000-shaft horsepower, giving a maximum speed of 22 knots. Her length was 650 feet with a gross registered tonnage of 24,733. She carried 1,412 tourist class passengers with a crew of 490.

Ocean Monarch *Ocean Monarch* was built as the *Empress of England* for Canadian Pacific at Vickers Armstrong of Newcastle. She was launched on the 9th May 1956 and on the 18th April 1957 made her maiden voyage from Liverpool to Montreal. Canadian Pacific sold the *Empress of England* to Shaw Savill for £5m on the 1st April 1970 and they renamed her the *Ocean Monarch*. After refitting to cruise status, she made her first voyage out of Southampton to the Mediterranean on the 16th October 1971. After several mechanical failures she became increasingly more expensive to operate and it therefore came as no surprise that Shaw Savill sold her for scrap. Her two near sisters, the *Empress of Britain* and the *Empress of Canada* are still sailing today, albeit under different names. Photographed in June 1975. **Technical Details -** Powered by geared turbines, driving twin screws, developing 30,000-shaft horsepower, giving a maximum speed of 21 knots. Her length was 640 feet with a gross registered tonnage of 25,971. She carried 1,372 passengers in one class with a crew of 464.

S S United States

The *United States* was by far the fastest of all the transatlantic liners, having a top speed of over 40 knots. She was built as the flagship of the United States Lines of New York and was delivered to her owners on 21st June 1952. Her maiden voyage from New York to Southampton commenced on 3rd July 1952 and broke all the North Atlantic records by sailing from the Ambrose Lightship to the Bishops Rock in just under 3 ½ days at an average speed of 33.39 knots, enabling her to win the coveted 'Blue Ribbon'. On the 8th November 1969 *United States* was withdrawn and laid up. There have been many failed attempts to reactivate her and she has even sailed across the Atlantic and back, albeit under tow. Her destination was Turkey to have her dangerous blue asbestos removed; she now remains laid up in Philadelphia, gently corroding away. A powerful photograph taken of her in October 1966.

Technical Details - Powered by Westinghouse geared turbines, driving quadruple screws, developing 240,000-shaft horsepower, giving a maximum speed of 40 knots. Her length is 990 feet with a gross registered tonnage of 53,329. She carried 1,928 passengers in three classes with a crew of 1,093.

S S France   The *France* was a symbol of luxury on the North Atlantic with her opulence and gastronomic delights. She was built for the Compagnie Generale Transatlantique, more commonly known as the French Line and cost $80m. On the 11th May 1960 she was launched by Madame Charles de Gaulle; the third ship to be named *France*. The building of the *France* was unusual, a lot of her construction was pre-fabricated in many factories across France and then transported to St Nazaire to be fitted together. There were no items of wood aboard her as everything was made of aluminium, formica and plastic. Her first class dining room, known as the Chambord, was one of the most exquisite rooms to be seen onboard any ocean liner. Many gourmets voted the *France*, 'the greatest restaurant in the World'. In 1972 she made her first World cruise, and as she was too big to pass through the Panama Canal, she had to circumnavigate South America. In July 1974 the French government stated that they would not subsidise the *France* anymore, which left the French Line with no options but to withdraw her and the *France* was laid up at an old pier in Le Havre. Several bids were made for her which proved to be unsuccessful until she was bought by the Oslo-based Norwegian Caribbean Lines and renamed the *Norway*. A Red Funnel Shearwater leaves Southampton for Cowes as tugs bring in *France* in May 1974.   **Technical Details** - Powered by geared turbines, driving quadruple screws, developing 160,000-shaft horsepower, giving a maximum speed of 35 knots. Her length is 1,035 feet with a gross registered tonnage of 66,348. She carried 2,044 passengers in two classes.

Flandre   The *Flandre* and her sister the *Antilles* were the first liners built for the French Line after the Second World War. She was built by Ateliers et Chantiers de France of Dunkirk for the Compagnie Generale Transatlantique and on the 31st October 1951 was launched and delivered to her owners. *Flandre* sailed on her maiden voyage from Le Havre to New York on the 23rd July 1952. Her maiden voyage was a disaster as she lost most of her power and had to limp into New York twenty two hours late, earning her the nickname of 'The Flounder' from the New York dockers. Taken off the New York to Le Havre run on entry of the *France* in 1962, she was overhauled, painted white and sent to the West Indies for cruising. The Costa Line became her new owners in 1968 and she was renamed firstly the *Carla C* and then the *Carla Costa..* In 1974 her ageing steam turbines were replaced with Stork-Werkspor diesel engines in an Amsterdam dockyard. She left the Costa Line in 1992 for Epirotiki Lines and received yet another name, *Pallas Athena.* In March 1994, whilst berthed at the terminal in Piraeus, she caught fire and was completely burnt out. Photographed in June 1961, from the collection of Barry J. Eagles.
Technical Details - Powered by Rateau geared turbines, driving twin screws, developing 44,000-shaft horsepower, giving a maximum speed of 22 knots. Her length was 600 feet with a gross registered tonnage of 20,469. She carried 784 passengers in three classes with a crew of 361.

Nieuw Amsterdam The *Nieuw Amsterdam* or the 'darling of the Dutch', as she was nicknamed, was built for the Holland/America Line by the Rotterdam Dry Docking Company. Queen Wilhelmina launched her on the 10th April 1937; but following her maiden voyage in May 1938 from Rotterdam to New York, few transatlantic voyages were made before the advent of the Second World War. After the German invasion of the Netherlands, the exiled Dutch Government placed the *Nieuw Amsterdam* at the disposal of the British Ministry of Transport. She was sent to Halifax, Nova Scotia to be refitted as a troopship and placed under the management of Cunard. After refitting she could carry 8,000 troops on a voyage. For the next six years she steamed 530,452 miles and carried 378,361 personnel. Her first Post-War voyage from Rotterdam to New York commenced on the 29th October 1947. In 1957 she was fully air-conditioned and given a grey hull and fitted with new boilers at the Wilton/Fijenoord Shipyard in Schiedam. Four years later it was decided that the *Nieuw Amsterdam* would only be used for cruising and her port of registry was changed to Willemstad, Curacao in the Dutch West Indies. At the end of 1973 *Nieuw Amsterdam* was withdrawn and sold for scrap and during March 1974 she arrived at Kaohsiung, Taiwan for demolition. Photographed in September 1968.
Technical Details - Powered by Parson's geared turbines, driving twin screws, developing 35,100-shaft horsepower, giving a maximum speed of 23 knots. Her length was 759 feet with a gross registered tonnage of 36,287. As built she carried 1,220 passengers in three classes with a crew of 694.

Daphne   *Daphne* started life as a cargo ship called the *Port Sydney* and was built for the Port Line by Swan Hunter and Wigham Richardson Ltd of Wallsend on Tyne. She was launched on the 29th October 1954. In 1972 she was sold to J C Carras and registered as the *Akrotiki Express* under the ownership of the Akrotiki Express Shipping Company and was rebuilt as a cruise ship at the Chalkis shipyard, Greece. She was luxuriously fitted out and renamed *Daphne* and on the 26th July 1974 she made her first Mediterranean cruise from Marseilles. In 1985 she was sold to Costa of Genoa and cruised to the Caribbean, Alaska and the Medierranean. In 1996 she left Costa for the Swiss company, Flotel, and is now named *Switzerland*.

Technical Details - Powered by two six-cylindered Doxford diesels, driving twin screws developing 13,200-brake horsepower, giving a maximum speed of 17 knots. Her length is 533 feet with a gross registered tonnage of 10,545. She carries 503 passengers in one class.

Kungsholm   *Kungsholm* was the last passenger ship to be built for the Swedish American Line; she was the fourth ship to be named *Kungsholm* and was built by John Brown on the Clyde. She was a handsome looking ship and was soon used exclusively as a luxury cruise liner. She was only to remain with Swedish American Line for ten years and apart from problems with air conditioning, she gave her owners little trouble. Swedish American decided to abandon passenger services in 1975 and she was sold to Flagship Cruises. Flagship hoped to capitalise on her excellent reputation and retained her name. *Kungsholm* was then Norwegian owned but registered in Monrovia. In January 1978, whilst on a Caribbean Cruise, she went aground in the Fort du France Bay in Martinique and was stuck fast for five days. This incident caused the end of Flagship Cruises as the salvage fees, repairs and disruption to the sailing programme proved very costly. In September 1978 she was sold to P&O Cruises and renamed *Sea Princess* (see page 26). Her white superstructure glows in this photograph from December 1974. **Technical Details** - Powered by Gotaverken diesel engines, driving twin screws, developing 27,700-brake horsepower, giving a maximum speed of 23 knots. Her length is 660 feet with a gross registered tonnage of 26,678. As built she carried 713 passengers in two classes with a crew of 438.

S A Vaal   This ship had the dubious distinction of being the last passenger ship built for the Union Castle Line. She was built as the *Transvaal Castle* by John Brown on the Clyde and on the 17th January 1961 was launched by Lady Cayzer, wife of the Chairman of British and Commonwealth Shipping Company. She was the first Union Castle Liner to carry tourist class passengers only and on the 18th January 1961 she left Southampton on her maiden voyage to Capetown. *Transvaal Castle* was transferred to South African Registry on the 3rd January 1966 and was renamed the *S A Vaal* for the South African Marine Corporation known as Safmarine. The *S A Vaal,* along with the former *Pretoria Castle* now renamed *S A Oranje* (see opposite page) also now under the South African Flag, worked in conjunction with the three remaining liners and the cargo ships, *Southampton Castle* and *Goodhope Castle*. She continued on the Cape run until she made her last arrival from the Cape to Southampton on the 10th of October 1977 after which she was sold to Carnival Cruises. She subsequently sailed from Southampton on the 29th October 1977 bound for Kobe where she was converted for full time cruising by Kawasaki Heavy Industries. *Festivale,* as she was now named, was delivered to her new owners on the 31st of August 1978 and on the 28th October that year she made her first Caribbean Cruise. She has now been bought by Premier Cruises and given an extensive overhaul to bring her up to requirements. She now sails as the *Island Breeze*. Photographed in July 1977.   **Technical Details** - Powered by Parson's geared turbines, driving twin screws, developing 44,000-shaft horsepower, giving a maximum speed of 23.5 knots. Her length is 760 feet with a gross registered tonnage of 32,697. As built she carried 728 passengers in one class with a crew of 426.

S A Oranje   *S A Oranje* was built as the *Pretoria Castle* for the Union Castle Line and she was the first of the two sisters built to replace War losses, her sister being the *Edinburgh Castle* (see page13). She was built by Harland and Wolff and launched on the 19th August 1947 by Mrs J Smuts, wife of Field Marshall Smuts, then Prime Minister of South Africa.   This was an unusual launch as Mrs Smuts was 6,000 miles away from Belfast, and a series of electrical impulses travelled from Capetown to crack a bottle of South African wine over the bows of the *Pretoria Castle*. She was transferred to the South African Registry on the 2nd February 1966 and renamed the *S A Oranje*.   She continued on this route until 1975 when she was sold for demolition at the Chin Tai Steel Enterprise of Kaohsiung, Taiwan, where she was broken up. This photograph, showing the very traditional lines of *S A Oranje*, was taken in July 1975.
Technical Details - Powered by geared turbines, driving twin screws, developing 35,000-shaft horsepower, giving a maximum speed of 22 knots. Her length was 747 feet with a gross registered tonnage of 28,705. As built she carried 755 passengers in two classes with a crew of 400.

Leonid Sobinov   *Leonid Sobinov* was built as the *Saxonia* (see page 8) for Cunard and sailed the North Atlantic route from Liverpool to Montreal until the end of 1962 when she was sent to her builders for refitting and renaming as *Carmania* (see page9).She was laid up in 1971 for two years and eventually sold to the Nikreis Maritime Corporation of Panama acting as agents for the Russian Black Sea Shipping Company of Odessa and renamed *Leonid Sobinov*. Leonid Sobinov was born in 1872 and died in 1934, he was a singer, actor and a director of the Bolshoi from 1905 to 1911. Like her sister she was marketed by CT Cruises and sent to Swan Hunter of South Shields for overhaul. On the 25th February 1974 she sailed from Southampton to Sydney on her maiden voyage for her new owners. In 1990 *Leonid Sobinov* was registered under the ownership of Transblasco Four Shipping Company Limited of Valetta, Malta. In 1995 she was withdrawn and laid up near Odessa where she still remains; it cannot be much longer before she makes her final journey to the scrapyard. Photographed in the hot summer of 1976.   **Technical Details** - Powered by geared turbines, driving twin screws, developing 24,500-shaft horsepower, giving a maximum speed of 20 knots. Her length is 608 feet with a gross registered tonnage of 21,846. She carries 929 passengers in one class.

Taras Shevchenko   *Taras Shevchenko* is the third of the Ivan Franko class, built for the Soviet shipping fleet by Mathias Thesen Werft of Wismar, East Germany and was launched on the 16th January 1965. The five members of the Ivan Franko class consisted of the *Ivan Franko* , *Aleksander Pushkin* (1965), *Taras Shevchenko*, *Shota Rustavelli* (1968 - see page46) and the final member *Mikhail Lermontov* (1972). Sadly the last of the class the *Mikhail Lermontov* was the first loss on a cruise from Sydney on the 16th February 1986. She struck rocks, was holed and sunk off Cape Jackson at the southern end of New Zealand's South Island. The only one of the class still in service is the *Aleksander Pushkin*, now renamed *Marco Polo*. Taras Shevchenko was born in 1814 and died in 1861, he was a great Russian poet, born in the Ukraine and was the son of a serf. *Taras Shevchenko*, the ship, was delivered on 26th April 1967 and was used mainly for cruising. After a 1974 refit she increased her tonnage but lost space for one hundred passengers in the process. On the 3rd October 1988 a refit was commenced at the Lloyd Werft of Bremerhaven, mainly to modernise her passenger accommodation and was returned to service on the 4th December 1988. At present the *Taras Shevchenko* is laid up and her next voyage will probably be one of no return. Photographed in her striking Russian colours in March 1976.
Technical Details - Powered by two seven-cylindered Sulzer-Cegielski diesels, driving twin screws developing 21,500-brake horsepower, giving a maximum speed of 20.5 knots. Her length is 578 feet with a gross registered tonnage of 20,027. She carries 750 passengers with a crew of 220.

Shota Rustavelli

Shota Rustavelli is the fourth of the Ivan Franko Class and was built for the Black Sea Shipping Company of Odessa by Mathias-Thesen-Werft of Wismar, East Germany and was launched in 1967. The Russian Merchant Fleet operated under three major divisions, the Black Sea Shipping Company of Odessa (of which the *Shota Rustavelli, Ivan Franko* and *Taras Shevchenko* belonged), the Far East Shipping Company of Leningrad (who owned the *Aleksander Pushkin*) and the Baltic Shipping Company of Leningrad (who owned the *Mikhail Lermontov*). Shota Rustavelli was another great Russian author and poet and is today remembered by a peak in the Bezengi Wall which is the highest part of the main Caucas chain. *Shota Rustavelli* was delivered to her owners on the 30th June 1968 and was mainly used for cruising from Tilbury and Southampton. She was chartered many times by the recently defunct CTC Lines, a Russian associate company. This company had brought cruising to the masses with their cheap, affordable cruising holidays. In 1975 *Shota Rustavelli* was refitted with a reduction of passenger accommodation and another refit in 1980 increased her gross registered tonnage. At present she is laid up and probably her next voyage will be to the scrapyard. Photographed in November 1976 shortly after a refit.

Technical Details - Powered by two seven-cylindered Sulzer-Cegielski diesels, driving twin screws developing 21,000-brake horsepower, giving a maximum speed of 20.5 knots. Her length is 577 feet with a gross registered tonnage of 20,499. She carries 650 passengers with a crew of 220.

Maksim Gorkiy   The *Maksim Gorkiy* was originally built as the *Hamburg* for the German Atlantic Line. As the *Hamburg*, her maiden voyage was from Cuxhaven to South America and commenced on the 28th May 1969. In 1973 *Hamburg*'s name was changed to *Hanseatic*. German Atlantic Line's owners ran into financial difficulties in December 1973 and they suspended operations causing the *Hanseatic* to be laid up. *Hanseatic* was then sold to the Robin International Corporation of New York acting on behalf of the Soviet State Shipping Company. On the 25th January 1975 she was transferred to the Black Sea Shipping Company of Odessa, and renamed *Maksim Gorkiy* and used for worldwide cruising. Maksim Gorkiy was born in 1868 and died in 1936, his correct name was Aleksey Maksimovich Peshkov. He was a Russian writer and politician and lived in exile on the Isle of Capri from 1906 to 1913, followed by a further period of exile in Italy from 1921 to1928. He was a personal friend of Josef Stalin. After a full refit in 1988 she returned to cruising, but on the 19th June the following year, hit ice whilst on a cruise from Iceland to the Gulf of Magdalen. Passengers and crew members were ordered to the lifeboats, but fortunately a hole was patched and the liner managed to reach Lloyd Werft at Bremerhaven for repairs. She has survived the recent upheavals in Russia and still cruises around the World. Seen in September 1978 complete with her unusual funnel. **Technical Details** - Powered by geared turbines, driving twin screws developing 22,660-shaft horsepower, giving a maximum speed of 22 knots. Her length is 639 feet with a gross registered tonnage of 24,981. She carries 600 passengers in one class.

Stefan Batory   The *Stefan Batory* was built for the Holland America Line as the *Maasdam,* sister to the *Ryndam* and was built by Wilton Fijenoord of Schiedam. The *Maasdam* was originally laid down in 1949 as a passenger/cargo vessel to be called the *Diemerdijk.* On the 5th April 1952 she was launched as the *Maasdam* and her maiden voyage from Rotterdam to New York commenced on the 11th August 1952. In 1968 she was sold to the Polish Ocean Lines of Gdynia, refitted and renamed *Stefan Batory.* By the late 1970s only two passenger ships remained on the transatlantic service, the *QE2* (see pageÖ) and the *Stefan Batory.* She made her final voyage from Montreal arriving at Gydnia on the 7th October 1987 and on the 26th March 1988 she made her last sailing under the Polish flag. In 1991 she sailed to Greece and is currently laid up in Chalkis. Photographed in September 1975.
Technical Details - Powered by General Electric geared turbine, driving a single screw developing 8,500-shaft horsepower, giving a maximum speed of 16.5 knots. Her length is 503 feet with a gross registered tonnage of 15,046. As the *Stefan Batory* she carried 779 passengers in one class.

Irpinia *Irpinia* was originally built as the *Campana* at Swan Hunter's in Newcastle. She cruised the seas for over half a century after her maiden voyage from Marseilles to Buenos Aires in December 1929. She became *Irpinia* after purchase by SIOSA Lines in 1955. Adriatico of Trieste refitted her in 1962 and her 33-year-old steam turbines were replaced by diesel engines, her two funnels were replaced by one domed funnel and her gross registered tonnage increased. After March 1970 she sailed purely as a cruise ship to Scandinavia from Tilbury, Southampton and Bremerhaven. *Irpinia*'s main business were weekly cruises from Genoa around the Mediterranean. She was withdrawn in 1981 and demolition commenced on the 2nd August 1983 at La Spezia by Cantiera Navali, Santa Maria. Photographed in July 1975. **Technical Details -** Powered by Fiat diesels, driving twin screws developing 16,000-brake horsepower, giving a maximum speed of 20 knots. Her length was 536 feet with a gross registered tonnage of 13,204. She carried 1,181 passengers in two classes.

Left: **Ascania** *Ascania* was another long-lived ship with a similar history to the *Irpinia*. She was built as the *Florida* for the Societe Generale de Transport Maritimes of Marseilles and was launched on the 14th January 1926. She was placed on the Marseilles to River Plate service and on one of these voyages in 1931 incurred major damage when she collided with the Aircraft Carrier, *H M S Glorious* off Gibraltar. In November 1942 Axis Aircraft sank her at Bone and it was another two years before she was salvaged, losing one funnel in the process. *Florida* was transferred to Chargeurs Reunis in 1951 and in 1955 she was bought along with her running companion, the *Campana*, by Sicula Oceanica of Palermo. Renamed *Ascania*, she was placed on the route to Central America bringing emigrants from the West Indies into Southampton. In 1966 *Ascania* was employed in full time cruising, but by now she was forty years old and she was withdrawn and sold for demolition at La Spezia two years later. Seen at Southampton's New Docks in September 1960, photograph from the collection of Barry J. Eagles. **Technical Details -** Powered by geared turbines, driving twin screws developing 6,500-shaft horsepower, giving a maximum speed of 14.5 knots. Her length was 490 feet with a gross registered tonnage of 9,536. She carried 1,115 passengers in two classes.

Above: **Leonardo da Vinci** *Leonardo da Vinci* was built as a replacement for the ill-fated *Andrea Doria* and was built for the Italia Line of Genoa by Ansaldo of Genoa and launched on the 7th December 1958. On the 17th June 1960 her maiden cruise commenced, but the true maiden voyage was from Genoa to New York, which commenced on the 30th June 1960. The *Leonardo da Vinci* was a very popular ship and nearly always carried a full compliment of passengers. On the 19th July 1965 she made her first voyage from Naples to the USA but with the advent of the super liners, *Michaelangelo* and *Raffaello*, she was replaced on the express route to New York. On the 23rd September 1978 she was laid up in La Spezia just to the south of Genoa and two years later caught fire burning for four days. Her remains were towed to a scrap yard in La Spezia, a sad end to a beautiful ship. **Technical Details -** Powered by Parson's geared turbines, driving twin screws developing 52,000-shaft horsepower, giving a maximum speed of 25 knots. Her length was 767 feet with a gross registered tonnage of 33,340. She carried 1,326 passengers in three classes with a crew of 580.

Achille Lauro The *Achille Lauro* was a ship that had more than its fair share of bad luck. Built as the *Willem Ruys* for Rotterdam Lloyd by De Schelde of Flushing. She was originally laid down in 1939 but due to the German occupation of Holland, it was not until the 1st July 1946 that the ship was launched. For ten years she plied between Rotterdam and Java until December 1957, when the Dutch East Indies became the Independent Republic of Indonesia. In January 1964 she was sold to the Lauro Line and a year later the ship was renamed the *Achille Lauro* and sent to the Cantieri Navali Riunite of Palermo for rebuilding and modernisation. In July 1984 *Achille Lauro* returned to cruising and whilst employed in this capacity, on the 7th October 1985, the ship was seized by Arab terrorists and one American tourist was killed. This incident led to the resignation of the Italian government. In 1987 *Achille Lauro* went to Star Lauro of Naples and on the 30th November 1994, her bad luck caught up with her for the final time. Whilst cruising in the Indian Ocean she caught fire and 979 people on board were forced to abandon ship, two passengers dying in the process. This colourful vessel is seen in July 1980.

Technical Details - Powered by 8 eight cylindered geared diesel engines, driving twin screws developing 32,000-brake horsepower, giving a maximum speed of 24 knots. Her length was 631 feet with a gross registered tonnage of 23,862. She carried 1,097 passengers in one class.

Fairsky   The *Fairsky* was built as an auxiliary aircraft carrier, the *U S S Barnes*. As the *Steel Artisan* she was launched on the 27th September 1941 but due to the Japanese attack on Pearl Harbour, on the 7th December 1941, she was taken over by the US Navy and completed as the *U S S Barnes*. In 1952 she was bought by the Vlasov Group (The V on the Sitmar Lines vessels funnel stands for Vlasov) and she was renamed *Castel Forte*. In 1957 work commenced on converting her to a passenger ship with air-conditioned accommodation and on completion of this work she was renamed *Fairsky* and registered in Monrovia for Sitmar. Her first voyage for her new owners was from Southampton to Sydney and commenced on the 28th June 1958. After a period cruising she was sold to the Penninsular Tourist Shipping Company of Manila as a floating hotel called the *Philippine Tourist*, but caught fire in November 1979 and was totally destroyed. Photographed in March 1974. **Technical Details** - Powered by General Electric Company geared turbine, driving a single screw developing 8,500 -haft horsepower, giving a maximum speed of 17.5 knots. Her length was 502 feet with a gross registered tonnage of 12,464. She carried 1,461 passengers in one class.

Fairstar *Fairstar* was originally built as Her Majesty's Troop Transport, *Oxfordshire*. She was the last troopship to be built for the British Government and was constructed for her owners Bibby Line of Liverpool by Fairfield Shipbuilding and Engineering Company Limited of Glasgow. In May 1963 she was chartered for six years to the Fair Line Shipping Corporation of Monrovia, part of the Sitmar Group. In March 1964 *Oxfordshire* was sold outright to Sitmar and renamed *Fairstar.* P & O purchased Sitmar cruises in July 1988 and *Fairstar* retained her name in the take-over. With the advent of the Safety and Life at Sea (SOLAS) regulations, P & O decided to withdraw her in January 1997 and sold her for demolition in India. A decision that Australian cruising passengers and ship lovers both regretted. Photographed in the New Docks in June 1974. **Technical Details** - Powered by geared turbines, driving twin screws developing 18,000-shaft horsepower, giving a maximum speed of 20 knots. Her length was 610 feet with a gross registered tonnage of 21,619. She carried 1,300 passengers in one class.

Sagafjord *Sagafjord* was built for the Norwegian American Line by Forges et Chantiers de la Mediterranee of La Seyne and she was launched on the 13th June 1964. She undertook trials during May 1965 and was delivered to her owners on 18th September 1965. For the next fifteen years she cruised and gained a marvellous reputation for good food and service. At the end of 1980 *Sagafjord* was sent to Blohm and Voss of Hamburg for refit and during the course of this another deck was added. Norwegian American Line had planned to merge with the Royal Viking Line in 1980 but nothing came of this and it was not until May 1983 that they found a buyer in the Cunard Line. *Sagafjord* and her running companion *Vistafjord* (see page 56) were transferred to the Cunard Line and registered in Nassau under the Bahamian flag. The only external signs of her new ownership were that her funnel was repainted in the traditional Cunard funnel colouring with Cunard written on her superstructure. She served with Cunard for over ten years and has now been bought by the Saga organisation which specialises in holidays for the over fifty's and now cruises out of Dover and Southampton under her new name *Saga Rose*. The delicate colours of *Sagafjord* are seen in August 1976. **Technical Details** - Powered by two nine-cylinder Sulzer diesels, driving twin screws developing 27,000-brake horsepower, giving a maximum speed of 20 knots. Her length is 620 feet with a gross registered tonnage of 24,474. She carries 509 passengers in one class with a crew of 350.

Vistafjord *Vistafjord* was one of the last traditional styled passenger liners built, and is one of the highest rated luxury ships in the World. Swan Hunter of Wallsend built her for the Norwegian American Line; she was launched on the 15th May 1972. Her maiden voyage to New York from Oslo commenced on the 22nd May 1973. Her history for the next few years was very similar to her running companion, *Sagafjord* (see page55). She was renowned for her World cruises and in May 1980, along with *Sagafjord*, was transferred to Norwegian American Cruises of Oslo. *Vistafjord, Sagafjord* and the goodwill of the Norwegian American Cruise Line was sold to Trafalgar House the owners of Cunard during May 1983 and transferred to the Bahamian flag and registered in Nassau. It was rumoured that her name would be changed to *Cunard Vista* but like her sister, her funnel colour was changed to Cunard's traditional red with the name Cunard added to her superstructure. At the end of 1999, after a refit, she will be renamed *Caronia*, reviving the name of an illustrious predecessor. Photographed in September 1978.   **Technical Details -** Powered by two nine-cylinder Sulzer diesels, driving twin screws developing 24,000-brake horsepower, giving a maximum speed of 20 knots. Her length is 627 feet with a gross registered tonnage of 24,116. She carries 690 passengers in one class with a crew of 390.

Calypso   *Calypso* was originally built as the *Southern Cross* (see page 33) and is a great survivor. Built for the Shaw, Savill and Albion Company by Harland and Wolff of Belfast, she was launched on the 17th August 1954. The *Southern Cross* served with Shaw, Savill and Albion for sixteen years and then was laid up in the River Fal. In January 1973 she was sold and renamed *Calypso* and chartered to Thompson Cruises by Ulysses Cruise Line. Her first voyage for her new owners began on the 25th April 1975 and was a Mediterranean Cruise. In 1980 *Calypso* was sold to the Eastern Steam Ship Line of Panama and renamed *Azure Seas*. A year later she was re-registered under the Western Steam Ship Line of Panama and undertook cruising around the World, mainly commencing from United States ports. She was registered under the ownership of the Azure Seas Incorporated and transferred to the Liberian flag in 1990. She is now named *Ocean Breeze* and her new owners are Premier Cruises, a firm that specialises in traditional elderly, mainly steam-powered ships. At forty-five years of age she has just passed the stringent 1997 Safety and Life at Sea regulations. It was once considered unlucky to change a ship's name; *Calypso* has certainly disproved this. Her hull catches the sunlight in April 1977. **Technical Details** - Powered by Parson's geared turbines, driving twin screws developing 20,000-shaft horsepower, giving a maximum speed of 20 knots. Her length is 604 feet with a gross registered tonnage of 14,776. She carries 821 passengers in one class.

Albatros   *Albatros* was built as the *Sylvania*, one of the Saxonia class liners for Cunard's Canadian service from Liverpool. She was the last of a quartet to be built and like her sisters came from John Brown's yard on the Clyde. She sailed on her maiden voyage from Greenock to Montreal on the 5th June 1957 and three weeks later sailed from Liverpool to Montreal. She continued on this service for the next ten years. In January 1968 *Sylvania* was sold to the Fairwind Shipping Corporation of Monrovia, part of the Sitmar organisation. She was renamed *Fairwind* and with her sister, the *Carinthia*, now renamed *Fairland*, was laid up in 101 berth in Southampton docks. *Albatros* was the only Sitmar Line ship that had been repainted in the new Sitmar House colours and was renamed *Sitmar Fairwind* before her sale. Then transferred to Princess Cruises and renamed *Dawn Princess* she was sold and is owned and operated by V Ships of Monaco and chartered to Phoenix Reisen Bonn, registered in the Bahamas and cruises around the World. Photographed in May 1994.

Technical Details - Powered by Parson's geared turbines, driving twin screws developing 24,500-shaft horsepower, giving a maximum speed of 20 knots. Her length is 608 feet with a gross registered tonnage of 24,803. She carries 906 passengers in one class.

Hanseatic *Hanseatic* was originally built as the *Empress of Japan* for Canadian Pacific. Built by Fairfield of Glasgow and launched on the 17th December 1929, she commenced her maiden voyage from Liverpool to Quebec on the 14th June 1930. On the 7th August 1930 she made her first voyage from Vancouver to Yokohama, being the service she was built for. During the Second World War she became a troopship and her name was changed to the *Empress of Scotland*. Her naval service ended on the 3rd May 1948. On the 13th January 1958 she was sold to the Hamburg Atlantic Line. The German shipping line had paid £1m for her and a refit at Howaldt Werke of Hamburg cost a further £1.4m. During the course of this refit she had her three funnels replaced by two of a more modern design. Her new name was *Hanseatic* and on the 19th July 1958 she made her first voyage under that name from Hamburg to New York. During the winter she cruised from New York to the Caribbean and from Cuxhaven to Scandinavia. On the 7th September 1966 whilst at New York's pier 84 she caught fire. The damage was so severe and expensive to repair that she was sold to Eisen and Metall of Hamburg for demolition. Photograph from the collection of Barry J. Eagles. **Technical Details** - Powered by geared turbines, driving twin screws developing 34,000-shaft horsepower, giving a maximum speed of 23 knots. As the *Hanseatic* her length was 673 feet with a gross registered tonnage of 30,030, and carried 1,252 passengers in two classes.

Australis   *Australis* was a ship with a long history; the Newport News Shipbuilding and Dry Docking Company built her as the *America* for the United States Line. *America* was launched on the 31st August 1939 and delivered to her owners on the 2nd June 1940. Her maiden voyage commenced on the 10th August 1940 and was a cruise from New York to the West Indies. On the 22nd July 1946 she made her first crossing of the Atlantic in the role for which she was intended. In November 1964 *America* was sold to the Chandris Group and renamed *Australis,* which means Australian Lady. After refit at Piraeus, she made her first voyage for her new owners from Piraeus to Sydney on the 20th August 1965. On the 18th November 1977 she made her last sailing from Southampton and in the following year she was sold to the American Cruise Line. She arrived in New York on the 19th May 1978 and was renamed *America*. Her final name was *American Star* and whilst being towed to Thailand to be used as a floating hotel, she ran into difficulties and went aground, breaking into two off Puerta Ventura in the Canary Islands. **Technical Details** - Powered by Parson's geared turbines, driving twin screws developing 37,400-shaft horsepower, giving a maximum speed of 24 knots. Her length was 723 feet with a gross registered tonnage of 26,485. As the Australis she carried 2,300 passengers in one class.

Europa   *Europa* was originally built as the *Kungsholm,* the third ship of that name, built for the Swedish America Line by De Scuelde of Vlissengen in Holland and was launched on the 18th October 1952 by Princess Sybilla of Sweden. *Kungsholm* went on the sales list in 1964 when the fourth and last *Kungsholm* (see page41) was launched. North German Lloyd of Bremen bought her and on the 16th October 1965 she was renamed *Europa.* This company had a new ship built for them in 1981 that took the *Europa's* name. The old *Europa* was sold that year to the Costa Line of Italy and renamed *Columbus.* In 1984 her name was changed yet again to *Costa Columbus* and in July 1984 she rammed a breakwater at Cadiz. She was badly holed, but safely landed her passengers and crew, before capsizing and was found to be damaged beyond economic repair. Photographed in August 1980.
Technical Details - Powered by Burmeister and Wain diesel engines, driving twin screws developing 18,600-brake horsepower, giving a maximum speed of 21 knots. Her length was 600 feet with a gross registered tonnage of 21,514. She carried 843 passengers in two classes.

Ellinis *Ellinis* has a similar history to her sister the *Britanis* (see page opposite), she was built as the *Lurline* for the Matson Navigation Company of San Francisco. As the *Lurline* she made her maiden voyage from San Francisco on a world cruise on the 27th January 1933. On the 11th December 1941 she became a troop transport for the U S Navy and remained in this employment for five and a half years, being finally returned to her owners on the 29th May 1946. In 1963 she was sold to Dimitri Chandris and refitted at Smiths Dock and Company Ltd, North Shields. She was renamed *Ellinis,* meaning Greek Lady, her sister *Monterey* took her name. *Ellinis* was used for cruising only until she was laid up in Piraeus on the 14th October 1980. In 1986 she was sold for demolition in Taiwan and some of her machinery was transported to the *Britanis*. Photographed in August 1969.

Technical Details - Powered by geared turbines, driving twin screws developing 25,000 shaft horsepower, giving a maximum speed of 19.5 knots. Her length was 632 feet with a gross registered tonnage of 18,564. She carried 1,398 passengers in one class with a crew of 350.

Britanis   The Bethlehem Shipbuilding Corporation of Massachusetts built *Britanis* as the *Monterey* for the Matson Navigation Company of San Francisco. She was launched on the 10th October 1931 and delivered to her owners on the 20th April 1932. After several changes in ownership and a distinguised record in the Second World War, Chandris bought her on the 30th June 1970 and after a refit at Piraeus she was renamed *Britanis,* which means British Lady. Recently she has been used as an accommodation ship for Cuban refugees and at present is laid up in Tampa Bay and it cannot be long before she suffers the same fate as her sisters. Her classic lines are viewed well in this photograph from May 1976.
Technical Details - Powered by geared turbines, driving twin screws developing 25,000-shaft horsepower, giving a maximum speed of 21.5 knots. Her length is 631 feet with a gross registered tonnage of 18,153. She carries 1,632 passengers in one class with a crew of 350.

INDEX

*Below: **Fedor Shalyapin**, built as the Cunard liner **Ivernia** and renamed the **Franconia** in 1963. She sailed on cruises from Southampton for her new owners, the Russian Black Sea Shipping Company, from 1973 and is currently laid up at Odessa. Photographed in June 1984.*

Bibliography

Fifty Famous Liners 1-3	Braynard & Miller	Patrick Stephens Ltd	1982-87
Emigrant Ships	Cooke Anthony	Carmania Press	1992
Shaw, Savill & Albion	De Kerbrech R	Conway Press	1986
Passenger Liners	Dunn Laurence	Adlard Coles Ltd	1961
Costa Liners	Eliseo & Piccione	Carmania Press	1997
Great Passenger Liners of the World Vol 3-6	Kludas Arnold	Patrick Stephens Ltd	1976-86
Great Passenger Ships of the World Today	Kludas Arnold	Patrick Stephens Ltd	1992
Great Passenger Liners - Of the P & O	McCart Neil	Patrick Stephens Ltd	1985
Of the Orient Line	McCart Neil	Patrick Stephens Ltd	1987
Atlantic Liners of the Cunard Line	McCart Neil	Patrick Stephens Ltd	1990
The Last Atlantic Liners	Miller William	Conway Press	1985
The Last Blue Water Liners	Miller William	Conway Press	1986
British Ocean Liners	Miller William	Patrick Stephens	1986
The Cruise Ships	Miller William	Conway Press	1988

As I bring this book to a close *Eugenio C*, now called *Edinburgh Castle* is in 102 berth on Southampton Docks, whilst the *Oriana* is being overhauled in the King George V Dry Dock. The winter is over and like migrating birds the *QE2*, *Oriana*, *Arcadia*, *Victoria* and *Sagarose* are starting to make their appearance for the summer cruising season. I hope that you have as much enjoyment viewing these magnificent leviathans as I have in producing this book.

Buses, Coaches & Recollecti

Henry Conn

© Henry Conn 2019

First published in 2019

British Library Cataloguing in Publication Data

A catalogue record for this book is available from the British Library.

ISBN 978 1 85794 531 7

Silver Link Publishing Ltd
The Trundle
Ringstead Road
Great Addington
Kettering
Northants NN14 4BW
Tel/Fax: 01536 330588
email: sales@nostalgiacollection.com
Website: www.nostalgiacollection.com

Printed and bound in the Czech Republic

Front cover: **AYLESBURY** Red Rover of Aylesbury built up a significant route network radiating from the town in the 1960s and '70s. The company's stock was mainly made up of second-hand vehicles and seen here on 14 May is former Safeguard of Guildford Willowbrook-bodied AEC Reliance EPH 189B, new in 1964 and acquired in 1971; it is leaving Aylesbury for the 14-mile journey to the village of Brill.

The No 1 UK single on this day was Abba's *Knowing Me Knowing You*. Bob Gell

Contents

Title page: **WOLLATON, NOTTINGHAM** On Trowell Road on 2 April is Trent No 745 (TRB 573F), an ECW-bodied Bristol FLF new in 1968. This and the similar TRB 568F to 572F spent their working lives at Ilkeston depot. During this time they had three owners: Notts & Derby from new until December 1971, Midland General from January 1972 to September 1976, and Trent from October 1976 to withdrawal. In this view No 745 has not had the Midland General NBC fleet name changed. On this day Red Rum won the Grand National for the third time. *Bob Gell*

Acknowledgements

The vast majority of the illustrations in this book are from the cameras of Bob Gell and Greg Booth. Without these views and the detailed notes on each, this book would not have been possible. My most sincere thanks to Bob – outstanding!

The PSV Circle Fleet Histories for the operators in this book and a number of issues of *Buses Illustrated* were vital sources of information.

1977 Happenings (1)

January
- Home Secretary Roy Jenkins announces he will be leaving House of Commons to become President of European Commission.

February
- Foreign Secretary Anthony Crosland dies after suffering a stroke.
- David Owen becomes Foreign Secretary.

March
- Government indicates that inflation has pushed up prices by almost 70% during the past three years.
- British Leyland announces intent to dismiss striking toolmakers at the company's Longbridge plant in Birmingham.
- Government wins vote of no confidence in House of Commons after Prime Minister James Callaghan makes deal with Liberal leader David Steel.

In 1977 Jimmy Carter was inaugurated as the 39th President of the United States.

On 27 March one of the world's worst air disasters occurred in the Canary Islands when two Jumbo jets collided on the airport runway, killing 583 people.

The Apple II and Commodore PET personal computers were first sold in this year, and the Atari 2600 gaming system was also released. NASA launched the 'Voyager 1' unmanned spacecraft, which later undertook fly-bys of Jupiter in 1979, and Saturn in 1980. NASA also launched the 'Voyager 2' unmanned spacecraft, which eventually did a fly-by of Jupiter in 1979, Saturn in 1981, Uranus in 1986 and Neptune in 1989.

On 26 June Elvis Presley performed in his last concert, dying in Memphis, Tennessee, on 16 August; more than 75,000 fans lined the streets of Memphis for his funeral. Other deaths in 1977 included actress Joan Crawford on 10 May (possibly aged 73, but her birth year has been disputed), comedian Groucho Marx, U-2 spy plane pilot Francis Gary Powers,

WARRINGTON Photographed on 1 March, this is Crosville No DFG39 (320 PFM), an ECW-bodied Bristol FS6G new in July 1961. *Author's collection*

On this day James Callaghan threatened to withdraw state assistance from British Leyland unless it put an end to strikes. Two weeks later the company's managers announced their intention to dismiss 40,000 toolmakers who had gone on strike at the Longbridge plant in Birmingham, which was costing the taxpayer more than £10 million a week.

actor Sebastian Cabot, crooner Bing Crosby, and opera star Maria Callas. On Christmas Day the world lost 'The Tramp', comic actor Charlie Chaplin.

Serial killer David Berkowitz was arrested in 1977. More commonly known as 'Son of Sam', he had killed six people and wounded seven over a period of a year in New York City. James Earl Ray, who had been jailed for the assassination of Martin Luther King Jnr, escaped from the Brushy Mountain State Prison in Petros, Tennessee, but was recaptured three days later. In France, the last execution by guillotine was carried out.

Djibouti and Vietnam joined the United Nations during 1977, Djibouti also gaining independence from France. In South Africa, anti-apartheid activist Steve Biko was killed in police custody after being arrested at a roadblock under the Terrorism Act. There were several bombings in South Africa that year, at Daveyton Police Station on the East Rand on 24 February, at a Pretoria restaurant on 7 March, at the Carlton Centre (the tallest building in Africa) in Johannesburg on 25 November, on a Pretoria-bound train on 30 November, and at Benoni railway station on the East Rand on 14 December. An unexploded bomb was found at a supermarket in Roodepoort on 22 December.

On 13 July New York City was plunged into a blackout that lasted for 25 hours and caused looting and other disorders in the city.

Pele, the Brazilian football legend, considered by some as the best soccer player of all time, retired from the sport in 1977.

Born this year were Orlando Bloom and Liv Tyler (*The Lord of the Rings*), Edward Furlong (*Terminator 2*), Sarah Michelle Gellar (*Buffy the*

SOUTHPORT Corporation took delivery of 12 MCCW-bodied Leyland PSUR1A/1Rs new in June and July 1968. They were numbered 59 to 70 (HWM 59F to 64F and JWM 65F to 70F). They were all transferred to Merseyside Transport on 1 April 1974, and seen here on 28 July is No 70 (JWM 70F) in Merseyside livery. *Author's collection*

On this day the first oil through the Trans-Alaska pipeline reached Valdez in Alaska.

Vampire Slayer), Piper Perabo (*Coyote Ugly*), and Brittany Murphy (*8 Mile*).

On television *Three's Company, Eight is Enough, CHIPs, The Love Boat* and *Soap* premiered during 1977. *Rocky* won the Academy Award for Best Picture, Peter Finch won the award for Best Actor for *Network*, and Faye Dunaway was voted Best Actress, also for *Network*. The first *Star Wars* movie was released, and other excellent films that year were *Annie Hall, Close Encounters of the Third Kind, Saturday Night Fever, The Goodbye Girl, Fun with Dick and Jane, A Bridge Too Far, Smokey and the Bandit* and *The Spy Who Loved Me*.

Without doubt 1977 was a standout year for music. Fleetwood Mac released their *Rumours* album, which has gone on to sell 40 million copies to date. The punk rock band the Clash released their self-titled debut album, and the Sex Pistols released their *Never Mind The Bollocks Here's The Sex Pistols* album. Other albums released included *Saturday Night Fever*, David Bowie's *Low* and *Heroes*, Meatloaf's rock opera *Bat out of Hell*, Iggy Pop's *Lust for Life*, Eric Clapton's *Slowhand*, Talking Heads' *77*, and ELO's *Out of the Blue*. Rock band Led Zeppelin played their last concert in the USA in July at Oakland, California.

How diverse and exciting 1977 was for music! The was funk, art punk, dance, and what would later become known as indie rock, while punk was still hitting its stride as new wave. Electronic music was in its exciting infancy – listen to Kraftwerk. Elsewhere, bands and artists of all stripes were making music that refused to fall into categorical line. The carefully boxed-in walls that for so long had confined popular music were crumbling, making room for new sounds and ideas that continue to inspire and influence the music we listen to today. That isn't to say that 1977 represented a complete break from tradition into uncharted musical waters. A list of the year's chart-topping singles reads like an infomercial selling you all the biggest '70s hits on one compact disc. The sounds of Abba's *Dancing Queen* filled every dance club, while other period mainstays like Andy Gibb, Barry Manilow, Fleetwood Mac and KC and the Sunshine Band also boasted songs that loomed large in the charts. New wave also began to emerge as a further evolution from punk. Stiff Records released the debut from an up-and-coming songwriting maverick named Elvis Costello, as well as *New Boots and Panties,* the debut album from Ian Dury and what would become his backing band, the Blockheads. Like Costello, Dury's music was born out of the UK's growing pub rock scene, and his debut mashed funk, early American rock and roll, dance and pop music into its own distinct concoction. The Jam also brought some sass and style to the yet-to-be-titled new wave movement. While 1977 gave rise to a host of fresh new musical faces, it also was the year that some old dogs tried their hands at some new tricks: Iggy Pop resurfaced, as did Steely Dan.

Enjoy the nostalgia…!

ARTICULATED DEMONSTRATOR On trial with South Yorkshire Passenger Transport Executive (SYPTE) on 17 July was this Leyland-DAB-Saurer articulated bus, carrying trade plate 2474 B. The bus was not used in service and it followed parts of the 56 route, but this was for demonstration purposes only, as it also followed other routes or bits of routes. The 56 was the favourite as the route included hill-climbing and was good for demonstrating the bus on bends. The public were invited to ride on it on demonstration runs and questionnaires were given out and collected. *Bob Gell*

On this day the No 1 single was So You Win Again *by Hot Chocolate.*

Photo	**DESTINATIONS**
1	**WOLLATON** (Title page)
2	**WARRINGTON**
3	**SOUTHPORT**
4	**SHEFFIELD**
5	**SHEFFIELD**
6	**SHEFFIELD**
7	**SHEFFIELD**
8	**SHEFFIELD**
9	**SANDTOFT**
10	**DONCASTER**
11	**DONCASTER**
12	**CHESTERFIELD**
13	**CHESTERFIELD**
14	**CHESTERFIELD**
15	**HALIFAX**
16	**HALIFAX**
17	**NOTTINGHAM**
18	**NOTTINGHAM**
19	**NOTTINGHAM**
20	**NOTTINGHAM**
21	**NOTTINGHAM**
22	**NOTTINGHAM**
23	**NOTTINGHAM**
24	**NOTTINGHAM**
25	**NOTTINGHAM**
26	**NOTTINGHAM**

SHEFFIELD Corporation purchased a batch of 26 Weymann-bodied AEC Regent Vs, which were delivered in April 1960 to replace trams on the penultimate route between Meadowhead and Sheffield Lane Top. They were 7435 to 7460 WJ, and this view of 7458 WJ, now a driver trainer, was taken on 17 July. I think the SYPTE livery is not as good on the eye as the Sheffield Corporation-liveried bus in the background. *Bob Gell*

SHEFFIELD In Pond Street bus station on the same day is East Yorkshire No 920 (BKH 920K), one of a batch of five Leyland PSU3B/4Rs new in May 1972 with Plaxton Panorama Elite II bodies. When new this bus featured the traditional 'Riviera Blue and Primrose' East Yorkshire coach livery – what a come-down to plain white! *Bob Gell*

Below: **SHEFFIELD** Another comparison between old and new liveries is possible in this view at Pond Street, also on 17 July. On the left, still in Sheffield Corporation livery, is No 240 (HWB 240J), a Park Royal-bodied Daimler CRG6LXB new in 1971. Next in line is a London DMS look-alike in PTE livery, No 1506 (OKW 506R), an MCW-bodied Leyland FE30 new in 1977. On the right, in PTE livery with a Silver Jubilee crest, is No 634 (WWJ 234G), a Park Royal-bodied Leyland PDR2/1 new in 1969. *Bob Gell*

Above: **SHEFFIELD** A large batch of Van Hool McArdle-bodied Volvo Ailsa B55-10s was delivered to SYPTE between April 1976 and February 1977. Representative of this batch is No 404 (LWB 404P), new in November 1976, seen in Pond Street bus station on the same occasion about to depart for Barnsley. In all, just over 1,000 Volvo Ailsas were produced, 890 of which had Alexander bodywork, with 64 having the unusual Van Hool McArdle Dublin-built body. The last significant number of Ailsas in service in the UK were operated by Cardiff Bus, which had 18 in regular service in 2007. I think the last of the SYPTE Van Hool McArdle examples lasted until October 1986. *Bob Gell*

Right: **SHEFFIELD** This is Yorkshire Traction No 252 (PWB 262R), a Duple-bodied Leyland PSU3E/4R new in March 1977. Seen here a few months later in July, No 252 is on a National Express service to Blackpool; note all the yellow stickers indicating a National Express service. *Bob Gell*

Right: **SANDTOFT** This is CWO 516K, a battery-electric bus built in 1971 by Crompton Morrison on an adapted Leyland 900FG chassis and bodied by Willowbrook. Initially used as a test bed and demonstrator, it ran for about three or four months in 1972/73 on the Birmingham Centrebus service. However, the restricted range of the batteries meant that it could not complete a full off-peak duty, so part way through a duty it had to return to the garage and be replaced by a diesel vehicle. The bus was acquired by SYPTE in 1975 and used intermittently on the Inner Circle in Doncaster. Withdrawn in 1979, it lingered in the training centre for several years until passing to a Barnsley dealer. This view was taken at Sandtoft Trolleybus Museum on 31 July. *Bob Gell*

The excellent Donna Summer single I Feel Love *was the No 1 single, and for me, the even better Emerson Lake & Palmer* Fanfare for the Common Man *was at No 3.*

DONCASTER The long-distance coach service run by Hall Brothers from Tyneside to Coventry ran until 1967, when Halls was taken over by Barton. Running as the X81 and X82, Barton coaches would run together as far as Sunderland, then the X81 would carry on to Newcastle and the X82 would follow the coast around to South Shields. In Doncaster working an X81 on 10 September is Barton No 1397 (ONN 280M), a Plaxton-bodied Leyland PSU3B/4R new in 1974. *Bob Gell*

On this day the last person convicted of murder to be beheaded by guillotine died in Marseilles.

DONCASTER On the same day at the same location is Greater Manchester Passenger Transp Executive (GMPTE) No 91 (KDB 678P), an ECW-bodied Leyland PSU3C/4T new in 1975. This combination of Leyland Leopard and ECW bodywork was an unusual purchase for GMPTE; No 9 spent much of its service life at Bolton and was sold to Chesterfield Transport in 1989, where it survived into the early 1990s. *Bob Gell*

Right: **CHESTERFIELD** Between June and July 1958 Chesterfield took delivery of 12 Weymann-bodied Leyland PD2/30s, Nos 213 to 224 (213 to 224 GRA). Working service 7 to Poolsbrook from Chesterfield bus station on 10 September is No 213 (213 GRA); this was the last of the batch to be withdrawn, in July 1978, and was sold for scrap four months later. *Bob Gell*

Left: **CHESTERFIELD** acquired from Merseyside Passenger Transport Executive in April 1977 ten MCW-bodied Leyland PSUR1A/1s. In service to Walton on Beetwell Street, also on 10 September, is No 59 (RKA 969G), which had only entered service with its new owner the previous month; it would be withdrawn after an accident in January 1984 and sold for scrap in March 1985. *Bob Gell*

CHESTERFIELD Heading along Beetwell Street on the same day is East Midland No 184 (GNN 184D), a Metro-Cammell-bodied Albion LR7 new in 1966. The LR7 had a single-plate clutch and a four-speed manual gearbox with synchromesh on third and top, with rear air suspension designed to provide a constant height (nearly 2 inches/5cm lower than the unladen height of the steel-sprung examples), regardless of loading. East Midland chose manual Lowlanders (having previously bought lowbridge Atlanteans) because the engine-braking available suited some of their hillier routes in the Peak District, notably route 4, Chesterfield to Doncaster, and route 17, Chesterfield to Matlock. The only modifications over a full service life of around 15 years were the removal of illuminated advertising displays from the first batch and the panelling over of the lower set of apertures in the radiator grille, as the engine was originally over-cooled in the upland climate in which these buses operated. *Bob Gell*

HALFWAY Also photographed on 10 September is Booth & Fisher's 334 NKT. This company purchased a quartet of Weymann dual-purpose-bodied AEC Reliances from Maidstone & District; this vehicle was acquired in 1973 and passed with the company to South Yorkshire Passenger Transport Executive in February 1976 and received SYPTE fleet number 1086 in 1978. *Bob Gell*

HALFWAY was the location of Booth & Fisher's depot, opened in 1962, where this view was taken. Leaving the depot for Killamarsh on the same day is HNU 786C, a Marshall-bodied AEC Reliance new in 1965. In the background is WRA 12, a Park Royal-bodied AEC Monocoach new in 1955. Booth & Fisher was operated by SYPTE as a separate entity for a number of years, although from April 1978 the vehicles had begun to be repainted and numbered into the SYPTE fleet. *Bob Gell*

NOTTINGHAM In 1965 North Western Road Car took delivery of five Alexander coach-bodied Leyland PSU3/3RTs, DDB 155C to 159C. All five passed to National Travel (North West) in February 1974 and were acquired by East Yorkshire in May 1975, entering service with their new owner the following month. Leaving Nottingham's Victoria bus station on 27 August en route to Cheltenham is No 156 (DDB 156C); sold in March 1978, it was purchased by Hulleys of Baslow in August of that year and sold for scrap by April 1980. *Bob Gell*

NOTTINGHAM Working the Central Area Service in Friar Lane on 5 March is Nottingham's No 724 (FAU 724L), a Leyland National new in 1973. It would be acquired by Red Rover in November 1978 and enter service before the end of the month. *Bob Gell*

NOTTINGHAM A few minutes later, working a 75 to Trent Bridge, is No 186 (MNU 186P), an NCME-bodied Daimler CRG6LX new in January 1976. This bus and a number of similar Daimlers were ordered with Willowbrook bodywork, but due to late delivery of the chassis the batch was sub-contracted to NCME. *Bob Gell*

The No 1 single on this day was the excellent When I Need You *by Leo Sayer.*

NOTTINGHAM This view taken in Sherwood Street on 2 August shows No 727 (GAU 727L), a Leyland National new in 1973, in the revised Nottingham livery; it would last longer in the Nottingham fleet, until 1980, and would be acquired by Red Rover in May of that year. *Bob Gell*

On this day Edward Furlong was born in Glendale, California; he is best known for his role as John Connor in Terminator 2: Judgement Day. *The next day, born in Sam Mateo, California, was Tom Brady, the NFL quarterback of the New England Patriots.*

NOTTINGHAM Leaving the city's Victoria bus station on 27 August is No 63 (GTO 63D) of Skill's of Nottingham, a Plaxton-bodied Leyland PSU3/3R new in May 1966; a short time after this view was taken, Davies Brothers of Pencader purchased the coach and it was retained in that fleet until September 1979. Via a further four operators the coach was acquired by Parfitt's of Rhymney Bridge for spares. *Bob Gell*

The No 1 album on this day was Going for the One by Yes, a band I was not particularly keen on.

NOTTINGHAM This is No 1201 (AFE 471B), one of four ECW-bodied Bristol RELL6Gs new to Lincolnshire in October-December 1964. It is leaving Victoria bus station for Grantham on 27 August. *Bob Gell*

A few days earlier Groucho Marx had died in Los Angeles, aged 86.

NOTTINGHAM During 1974 Midland Red purchased 20 Ford R1014s with Plaxton Derwent bodywork; they were the final batch of Fords acquired by Midland Red and entered service from April 1974. No 370 (PHA 370M) is leaving Victoria bus station on that same August day working service X99 to Birmingham via Tamworth and Ashby-de-la-Zouch. No 370 entered service in May 1974 from Tamworth depot and remained there until transfer in August 1977 to Wellington. Withdrawn from service in May 1979 the bodywork was shortened and it returned to service in Redditch in October of that year. Transferred to Evesham in January 1981, it moved to Worcester in September 1983, remaining there until February 1990, and is now in preservation. *Bob Gell*

NOTTINGHAM East Midland took delivery of a batch of 14 Alexander-bodied Albion LR7s in 1963, and representing this batch is No D269 (169 NVO). Of note is the fact that the Albion Lowlanders operated in England were badged as Leyland, and when this view was taken on 27 August at Victoria bus station No 169 still retained the Scottish flag at the top of the front grille; many had disappeared later in their service life. *Bob Gell*

NOTTINGHAM Working service 45 at Loughborough Road, West Bridgford, en route to Wollaton Park on 2 August is No 83 (83 RTO), a 1963 NCME-bodied Daimler CRG6LX. No 83 was one of four from the 1963 batch of Daimlers that were rebodied by NCME (this example in December 1975) due to the late delivery of new buses. *Bob Gell*

At the cinema at this time was the horror film The Hills have Eyes.

1977 Happenings (2)

March (Continued)
* Budget reduces income tax from 35p in the pound to 33p in the pound.

April
* British Aerospace formed to oversee nationalised aviation industry.

May
* Her Majesty the Queen launches HMS *Invincible* at Barrow-in-Furness.
* Silver Jubilee review of police at Hendon.
* Silver Jubilee Air Fair at Biggin Hill.
* Her Majesty the Queen starts Silver Jubilee tour of United Kingdom in Scotland, and opens new terminal building at Edinburgh Airport.
* M5 motorway is completed with opening of final stretch near Exeter by Prime Minister James Callaghan.

June
* Jubilee celebrations held throughout the United Kingdom to celebrate 25 years of Queen's reign. Tuesday 7 June is granted as additional public holiday and, although weather is generally cool and damp, street parties and other celebrations are much enjoyed

July
* Don Revie resigns after three years as manager of England national football team – and quickly accepts offer to become manager of United Arab Emirates football team.
* Tommy Docherty is dismissed as manager of Manchester United – his replacement is Dave Sexton from Queen's Park Rangers.

August
* Stage Three voluntary one-year pay restraint introduced by Government.

NOTTINGHAM This is Finney No 1 (XTO 249), a Park Royal-bodied AEC Regent V. It was new to Nottingham in November 1956, and acquired by J. Finney of West Bridgford, initially for preservation in March 1976, but was licensed as a PSV from March 1977. No 1 worked a service across West Bridgford for a year and was then sold to SYPTE for spares, and scrapped a month later.
Bob Gell

NOTTINGHAM Delivered to Midland General in May 1964 was 1385 R, an ECW coach-bodied Bristol RELH6G. During January 1977 the coach was sold to Trent with fleet number 266, and this view was taken at Mount Street bus station on 5 March. A few months later, during September, No 266 was withdrawn from service by Trent and sold in December to Bracebridge Heath for spares recovery. *Bob Gell*

Five days after this view was taken the rings of Uranus were discovered.

COVENTRY Leaving the city's Pool Meadow bus station is West Midlands Passenger Transport Executive (WMPTE) No 53Y (KKV 53G), an East Lancashire-bodied Daimler CRG6LX new to Coventry in 1969. Note the unusual sliding vents on the lower deck and the rotovents on the upper deck. *Bob Gell*

COVENTRY Plaxton and Duple built the majority of bodies for the Bedford YMT, though Van Hool and Van Hool McArdle accounted for more than 130. New to Smith of Bedfont and seen here on 3 August in the fleet of Sabre Coaches of Coventry is VMJ 957S, with a Van Hool McArdle body. A Bedford YMT with Plaxton Supreme bodywork cost £18,311, almost £5,000 less than an AEC Reliance, and the first to buy the YMT was Harry Shaw Ltd of Coventry in 1976. *Bob Gell*

August (Continued)
- RMS *Windsor Castle* makes Union Castle Line's final passenger/mail voyage from Southampton to Cape Town.
- Ron Greenwood, general manager of West Ham United, appointed temporary manager of England national football team.
- New-style smaller pound note is introduced.

September
- Figures indicate that for first time total sales of foreign cars have exceeded those for British models on home market.
- Freddie Laker launches 'Skytrain' airline – charging £59 from Gatwick to New York compared with normal fare of £186.

October
- Undertakers go on strike in London.
- Former Liberal leader Jeremy Thorpe denies allegations of attempted murder.

November
- National strike by firefighters starts; they seek a 30% wage rise.
- HRH Princess Anne gives birth to son, making Her Majesty the Queen a grandmother for first time.
- British Airways starts regular supersonic Concorde service between London and New York.

Left: **COVENTRY** Passing in front of Coventry's Council House on 3 August is West Midlands No 272Y (XVC 272), a Metro-Cammell-bodied Daimler CVG6 new to the city in 1959. Coventry Corporation buses were transferred to WMPTE on 1 April 1974, but in this view No 272Y still retains its final Coventry livery, which had been introduced in 1970. *Greg Booth*

Right: **LOUGHBOROUGH** This interesting line-up of former Leicester City Transport buses, photographed on 12 March, is at Yeates, a dealer in Derby Road, Loughborough. On the left is 221 DRY, a Park Royal-bodied AEC Bridgemaster new to Leicester in September 1962. After withdrawal from service in September 1971, after only nine years in the fleet, No 221 was acquired by Roberts of Cefn Mawr, where it remained until sold to Yeates in September 1976. Just after this view was taken the bus was sold to Castle Point Bus Company, then to Vintage Bus Company, but never operated and used as a store shed. Former Leicester Nos 188 and 190 (DBC 188C and DBC 190C) are East Lancashire-bodied AEC Renowns new in August 1965. After withdrawal they were acquired by Yeates in December 1976 and both were sold on, No 188 to Red House Motor Services in May 1977 and No 190 to Taylors of Sutton Scotney in November 1977, and now in preservation. *Bob Gell*

Above left: **LEICESTER** Working service 42 to Welton Road on 3 August is Leicester's No 75 (CJF 75C), one of a batch of ten East Lancashire-bodied Leyland PD3A/1s that were delivered new between January and March 1965; No 75 was sold to Castle Point Bus Company in November 1980 and sold again for scrap only seven months later. *Greg Booth*

Above right: **LEICESTER** The first Scania BR111DH to be purchased by Leicester was No 266 (PJF 266M), bodied by MCW and new in April 1974. This view, also taken on 3 August, shows the bus in Silver Jubilee livery. About to overtake it is No 258 (258 ERY), a Park Royal-bodied Leyland PD3A/1 new in January 1963; it would be sold to Powell of Wickersley in March 1978, remaining in that fleet until May 1983. *Greg Booth*

Left: **LEICESTER** At Humberstone Gate on 12 March is Leicester No 12 (PJF 12R), a Willowbrook Spacecar coach-bodied Leyland PSU3D/4R new in November 1976. The Spacecar was offered in three lengths, 10, 11 and 12 metres, and built on AEC, Bedford, Leyland, Seddon and Volvo chassis, the last two for the export market. Sadly the Spacecar did not take the market by storm and operators did not like the futuristic styling. Only 93 were built for customers, including two for the export market, and production ceased in November 1978, the National Bus Company being the design's largest customer. No 12 was sold to a dealer in August 1985, and by August 1987 was with De Courcey Travel of Coventry. *Bob Gell*

Left: **LEICESTER** City Transport bought 35 single-deck Metro-Scanias, and following their success bought 68 double-deck Metropolitans in several batches between 1974 and 1977 (and a handful of second-hand examples for further service and spare parts), both in dual-door configuration and a final batch of five with a single door in 1977. Twenty were acquired in February and March 1976, and representative of this batch, at the same location as the previous view, is No 167 (LNR 167P). The production of Metropolitans was finally terminated in 1978, the last examples going to Reading Transport, with two built to dual-purpose specifications with high-speed rear axles to operate the express X1 service to Aldgate, London. In all 662 Metropolitans were built. *Bob Gell*

Right: **NORTHAMPTON** Leaving the town's Greyfriars bus station on 14 May is No 251 (BNH 251C), a Roe-bodied Daimler CVG6 new in 1965. *Bob Gell*

The truly excellent First Cut is the Deepest, *written by Cat Stevens in 1965, became a No 1 hit for Rod Stewart a few days after this view was taken.*

Below: **AYLESBURY** In March 1962 Red Rover of Aylesbury placed in service 27 WKX, a new AEC Bridgemaster with a 74-seat rear-entrance body. This view was taken at Red Rover's Aylesbury depot on 14 May. The AEC Bridgemaster was by no means an overwhelming success and only a total of 179 were built in about six years of production. Next in line is DAU 383C, a Weymann-bodied AEC Renown new to Nottingham in June 1965 and acquired by Red Rover in July 1976, entering service three months later; it would be scrapped in September 1980. *Bob Gell*

Above: **NORTHAMPTON** On 14 May we see ORB 862E of Wesleys of Stoke Goldington, a Plaxton-bodied Ford R226. It was new in March 1967 to Depot Coaches Limited of Long Eaton, passing to J. R. Davies (J.R.D. Coaches) of London SW11 in October 1971, then to J.R.D. Travel Limited in July 1974. It came to Wesleys in June 1975 and remained until December 1981. By March 1984 it was in the fleet of Wright's Coaches of Connah's Quay, where it saw service for another two years. *Bob Gell*

AYLESBURY Leaving the town's bus station for Waddesdon on the same day is Red Rover's JPP 11C, a Marshall-bodied AEC Reliance new to the company in 1965. Aylesbury had a fantastic club called Friars and I saw a number of bands there during 1977, included Sassafras on 1 January, Greenslade on 12 February, Procol Harum on 12 March, Motorhead on 6 August and, best of all, Camel on 25 August. *Bob Gell*

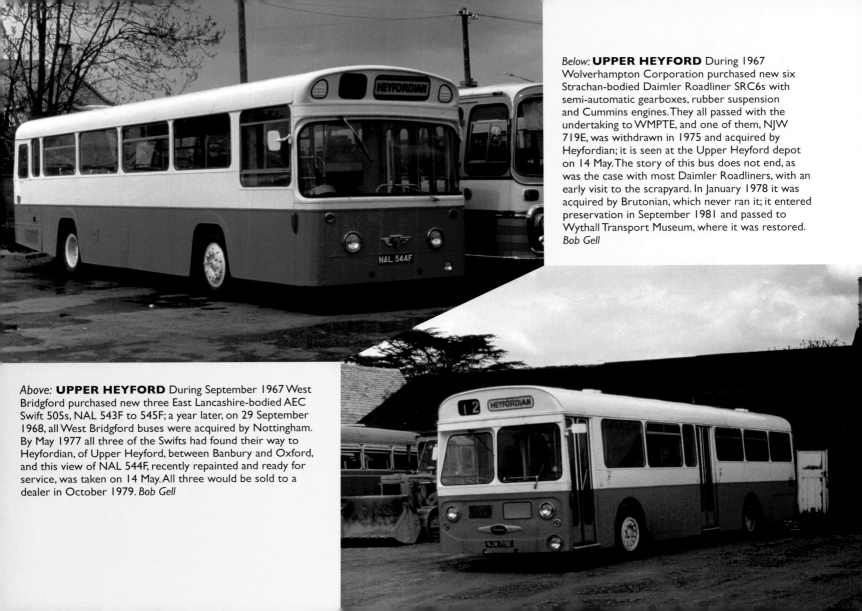

Below: **UPPER HEYFORD** During 1967 Wolverhampton Corporation purchased new six Strachan-bodied Daimler Roadliner SRC6s with semi-automatic gearboxes, rubber suspension and Cummins engines. They all passed with the undertaking to WMPTE, and one of them, NJW 719E, was withdrawn in 1975 and acquired by Heyfordian; it is seen at the Upper Heyford depot on 14 May. The story of this bus does not end, as was the case with most Daimler Roadliners, with an early visit to the scrapyard. In January 1978 it was acquired by Brutonian, which never ran it; it entered preservation in September 1981 and passed to Wythall Transport Museum, where it was restored. *Bob Gell*

Above: **UPPER HEYFORD** During September 1967 West Bridgford purchased new three East Lancashire-bodied AEC Swift 505s, NAL 543F to 545F; a year later, on 29 September 1968, all West Bridgford buses were acquired by Nottingham. By May 1977 all three of the Swifts had found their way to Heyfordian, of Upper Heyford, between Banbury and Oxford, and this view of NAL 544F, recently repainted and ready for service, was taken on 14 May. All three would be sold to a dealer in October 1979. *Bob Gell*

UPPER HEYFORD Photographed on the same occasion, in Heyfordian livery, is LRS 142 (left), a Duple-bodied Bedford SB3 new to Summers of Aberdeen in 1958. Alongside is former Southdown No 1141 (XUF 141), a Weymann Fanfare-bodied Leyland PSUC1/2 delivered in March 1960. Acquired by Heyfordian in 1973 and still in use in 1980, notably still in Southdown green, it survives today in preservation. *Bob Gell*

UPPER HEYFORD During 1963 North Western Road Car took delivery of a large batch of Willowbrook-bodied AEC Reliances, numbered 917 to 951 (VDB 917 to 951). At Heyfordian's depot on 14 May, and looking slightly the worse for wear, is VDB 933. *Bob Gell*

On this day England football international Bobby Moore retired.

Below: **CAMBRIDGE** Percivals Motors (Oxford) Limited, Percivals Motors (Cambridge) Limited and Premier Travel Services Limited of Cambridge operated a joint coach service for many years linking the two university cities. In Drummer Street bus station on 1 August is CBW 535R, a Plaxton-bodied Bedford YMT new to Percivals in May 1977. *Greg Booth*

Above: **CAMBRIDGE** Working a local service in the city on 1 August is Eastern Counties No LFS54 (54 CPW). Delivered new to Eastern Counties in July 1963, it was a Bristol FS5G with ECW bodywork. Withdrawn from service in 1981, it was one of the final batch of LFS class vehicles to remain in service with the company. Allocated to Cambridge during most of the 1970s, No LFS54 was latterly allocated to Yarmouth. Upon withdrawal it was acquired by Ben Jordan of Coltishall, then became a mobile home/publicity vehicle for a peace campaign. Later acquired by Viv Carter of Carters Coaches, Ipswich, it has since passed into preservation. *Greg Booth*

Below: **CAMBRIDGE** The Scottish Bus Group had a total of 109 Bristol VRs, 25 of which were the long VRT/LL type. These buses proved unreliable with the SBG and during 1971 Alexander Midland exchanged its 15 VRTs for 15 Eastern National Bristol FLFs with Gardner engines. The SBG was determined to get rid of its unloved and uncared for VRTs, and Eastern Counties ultimately took 33, some being of the troublesome VRT/LL 33-foot-long variety, and their mechanical condition on arrival was poor. Arriving at Drummer Street on 1 August is No VR331 (NAG 589G), an ECW-bodied Bristol VRT/SL6G new to Western SMT in 1969 and acquired by Eastern Counties in May 1973. *Greg Booth*

Above: **CAMBRIDGE** Premier Travel Ltd was founded on 1 January 1936 by three undergraduates from Cambridge University, formed from a combination of three operators, Undergraduate Roadways, Harston & District and Royal Blue Cambridge. Premier Travel of Cambridge operated express services around the country as well as stage carriage services in the Cambridge area. In Drummer Street bus station on 1 August, due to work from Cambridge to Bedford and Northampton, is GER 501E, one of two Alexander-bodied AEC Reliances new in May 1967. *Greg Booth*

Right: **LONG MELFORD** Theobald's Coaches started running buses in the 1920s and was based in the small town of Long Melford. The company operated in the area around Sudbury, Haverhill and Bury St Edmunds, and its office and garage was on Main Street; however, due to lack of space a number of buses were parked in the street or the former railway station yard. Duple-bodied Bedford YRT LBJ 65P (left) was new to Theobald's in 1975 and became a regular performer on the stage carriage services such as the indicated service to Sudbury. The Weymann-bodied AEC Renown beside it, DAU 364C, had been new to Nottingham in April 1965 and was acquired by Theobald's in March 1977; this view was taken on 1 August. *Bob Gell*

FENSTANTON Preparing for a journey to St Ives on 1 August is Whippet's HFL 672L, an NCME-bodied Leyland AN68/2 acquired new by the company in February 1973 and withdrawn from service in January 1984. This bus was acquired by Delaine and remained in that fleet until acquired for preservation in July 1997. *Bob Gell*

COLCHESTER During April 1975 Colchester Corporation took delivery of six ECW-bodied Leyland AN68/1Rs, Nos 55 to 60 (JHK 495N to 500N), and this view of Nos 56 and 57 was taken on 1 August. No 57 was withdrawn and sold in January 1989, and No 56 passed to Ensign for scrap in September 1989. *Greg Booth*

Gloucestershire

WINCHCOMBE At the depot of Castleways Coaches in Winchcombe on 3 August is Alexander-bodied Dennis Loline RDB 882 (right), a 1961 Dennis Loline III that had been purchased new by North Western. Upon the break-up of that company, it passed to SELNEC, following which it spent a short time in the fleet of Black Prince of Morley, before arriving at Castleways. On withdrawal in 1981 it is believed to have been exported to Italy. On the left is 405 COR, an Alexander-bodied Dennis Loline III new to Aldershot & District in 1961 and purchased by Castleways in 1971. *Bob Gell*

SLIMBRIDGE At the Slimbridge Wildfowl Trust near Dursley on 15 July is 974 WAE of Morris Brothers of Swansea, an ECW-bodied Bristol RELH6G new to Bristol in June 1964. As Bristol No 2128 it was acquired by Western National in June 1974 and sold to North of Sherburn in January 1977. Morris Bros purchased the coach in May 1977, and it remained with the company until May 1984, when it was acquired by Capitol Coaches of Cwmbran. *Bob Gell*

Below: **CHELTENHAM** On the same day we see Black & White No 114 (MDF 114P), one of a batch of eight Plaxton-bodied Leyland PSU3C/4Rs new in 1976. Black & White became part of National Travel (South West) on 1 January 1974; this batch carried the National Travel white livery but retained the Black & White fleet name. *Bob Gell*

Above: **CHELTENHAM** In October 1965 Midland Red took delivery of No 5815 (CHA 115C), a Duple Northern Commander-bodied Leyland PSU3/4R. In service from Bearwood in April 1966, No 5815 was reallocated to Banbury from February 1967, where it remained for most of its service life with Midland Red. Withdrawn in November 1975, it was acquired by National Travel (South West), in whose livery and numbered 215 it can be seen at Cheltenham coach station on 17 March. Three months later the coach was withdrawn; interestingly, just under two years later Fieldsend of Salford acquired it, and it remained with that company for a year. Also in view is YTX 322H, a Plaxton-bodied Leyland PSU3A/4RT new to Rhondda in 1970 and acquired by Western Welsh on 1 January 1971; this coach passed to Greenslades in January 1972, then to National Travel (South West) in October 1974. *Bob Gell*

No 1 Records

January
When a Child is Born   Johnny Mathis
Don't Give Up On Us   David Soul

February
Don't Cry For Me Argentina   Julie Covington
When I Need You   Leo Sayer

March
Chanson D'Amour   Manhattan Transfer

April
Knowing Me, Knowing You   Abba

May
Free   Deniece Williams
I Don't Want To Talk About It/
First Cut Is The Deepest   Rod Stewart

June
Lucille   Kenny Rogers
Show You The Way To Go   Jacksons

July
So You Win Again   Hot Chocolate
I Feel Love   Donna Summer

August
Angelo   Brotherhood of Man
Float On   Floaters

September
Way Down   Elvis Presley

October
Silver Lady   David Soul
Yes Sir, I Can Boogie   Baccara

November
The Name of the Game   Abba

December
Mull of Kintyre/Girls' School   Wings

CHELTENHAM Leaving the coach station on that same March day is Lincolnshire Road Car No 1438 (PFE 715K), a dual-purpose ECW-bodied Bristol RELH6G new in May 1972. Visible to the right working 'The Eastlander' to Ipswich is Premier Travel of Cambridge's VER 262L, an Alexander-bodied AEC Reliance new in 1973. *Bob Gell*

SWINDON In August 1975 Thamesdown Transport purchased new five ECW-bodied Bristol RESL6Gs, numbered 166 to 170 (JMW 166P to 170P). On Fleming Way on 17 March is No 168 (JMW 168P); by October 1987 all five had been sold to Busways Travel Services of Newcastle. *Greg Booth*

Three days earlier the Government had revealed that inflation had increased prices by nearly 70% over the previous three years.

SWINDON Ten Metro-Cammell-bodied Daimler CRG6LXs were purchased new by Swindon Corporation in October and November 1973, numbered 156 to 165 (NHR 156M to 165M). Leaving Swindon bus station on 17 February for a journey to Princess Margaret Hospital is No 158 (NHR 158M); this bus was sold through a dealer in January 1990 to Martindale Coaches of Ferryhill and by October 1991 it was in the fleet of Durham City Coaches. *Greg Booth*

BRISTOL This excellent view taken at Temple Meads railway station on 9 January shows three differing ECW bodywork designs for the Bristol RE. On the left and right of the picture are Nos 2045 and 2047 (KHW 314E and KHW 316E), Bristol RELH6Ls new in June 1967 and July 1967 respectively. Second from left is No 2058 (TAE 419G), another Bristol RELH6L new in July 1969, and beside it is No 1336 (OAE 958M), a Bristol RELL6L new in November 1973. *Greg Booth*

The rock band Toto was formed in Los Angeles on this day.

BRISTOL New to Western National in 1963 was 820 KDV, an ECW-bodied Bristol FLF6B; it was acquired by Bristol Omnibus in January 1970 and given the fleet number 7317. This view was taken in Bath on 5 August, and No 7317 would remain in the Bristol fleet until sold for scrap in December 1978. *Greg Booth*

Three days later the Queen and Duke of Edinburgh visited Bath during their Silver Jubilee tour of the UK.

1977 Happenings (4)

December
- Ron Greenwood confirmed as manager of England national football team.
- Queen opens extension of London Underground Piccadilly Line from Hatton Cross (terminus since 1975) to Heathrow Central, bringing direct Underground link to London Airport..

WESTON-SUPER-MARE An unusual purchase by Bristol Omnibus was No 301 (PHU 647M), a Leyland 440EA with Ascough Clubman 17-seat bodywork new in 1973 and seen on the Weston-super-Mare depot forecourt on 6 August. The minibus spent much of its time operating a city centre shoppers' service in Gloucester and was withdrawn in 1982. *Bob Gell*

1977 Arrivals & Departures

Births

Michelle Behennah	Model	7 January
Orlando Bloom	Actor	13 January
Hayley Tamaddon	Actress	24 January
Ben Ainslie	Competitive sailor	5 February
Colin Murray	Radio DJ	10 March
Adrian Morely	Rugby League footballer	10 May
Samantha Morton	Actress	13 May
Rachael Stirling	Actress	30 May
Joel Ross	Radio DJ	31 May
Angela Beesley	Co-founder of Wikia	3 August
Danny Griffin	Footballer	10 August
Gavin Meadows	Freestyle swimmer	8 September
Alistair Griffin	Singer/songwriter	1 November
Kavana (Anthony Kavanagh)	Singer	4 November
Peter Phillips	Son of HRH The Princess Royal	15 November
Paul McVeigh	Footballer	6 December
Matt Baker	Television presenter	23 December

Deaths

Anthony Eden	Politician	(b1897)	14 January
Peter Finch	Actor	(b1916)	14 January
Anthony Crossland	Politician	(b1918)	19 February
Madeline Dring	Composer/actress	(b1923)	26 March
Stephen Boyd	Actor	(b1931)	2 June
Lady Olave Baden-Powell	Chief Girl Guide	(b1889)	25 June
Henry Williamson	Writer	(b1895)	13 August
Edward Sinclair	Actor	(b1914)	29 August
Leopold Stokowski	Musician	(b1882)	13 September
Marc Bolan	Musician	(b1947)	16 September
Terence Rattigan	Playwright	(b1911)	30 November
Charlie Chaplin	Actor	(b1889)	25 December

WESTON-SUPER-MARE On the seafront on 6 August is Bristol No 7900 (841 SHW), an ECW-bodied Bristol FLF6B new in August 1964. Following an accident in March 1976, the bus was converted to open-top form; the only open-top FLF in the Bristol fleet, it is now in preservation. *Bob Gell*

WESTON-SUPER-MARE Wallasey Corporation's No 15 (HHF 15) was delivered to the company's Seaview Road depot and registered in March 1960. In order to be able to operate as a one-person bus it was fitted with a door on the stairs, which could be shut and locked to prevent upstairs access; other buses had this door removed, but No 15 retained it. The bus was transferred to Merseyside PTE and received fleet number 215, remaining in the PTE fleet until the end of 1973. It was then sold to Primrose Coaches of Bedminster in April 1974 and remained in service there until 1996, latterly on schools contracts, providing Primrose Coaches with some 23 years of service; it was then purchased for preservation and is currently in the fleet of Merseyside Transport Trust. This view of HHF 15 was taken in Weston-super-Mare on 6 August. *Greg Booth*

TAUNTON On the forecourt of Taunton bus depot on 6 August are two ECW-bodied Bristol FLF6Gs, Nos 2079 (BDV 258C), new in 1965, and 2024 (404 PTA), new in 1963. *Bob Gell*

SPARKFORD Nearest the camera is 312 KYC, a Duple Super Vega-bodied Bedford SB new to Bowerman of Taunton in March 1961. The coach was acquired by Wake's of Sparkford in December 1964 and remained there until July 1989. In 1965 Wake's won the contract for the main replacement bus service for the Somerset & Dorset railway line from Glastonbury to Blandford, closed the following year, but at the last moment Wake's withdrew their licence application and the contract was retendered and eventually awarded to Somervale Coaches. Wake's had ordered Bedford VAM5s in 1965 with Willowbrook dual-purpose bodywork to operate the service, and seen on the right is FYC 126C. The Bedford VAM5s were generally used on the main Yeovil to Shepton Mallet service and, as they were fitted with coach seats, on excursions at weekends and during the summer. This bus was withdrawn in July 1989 and became a mobile home. *Greg Booth*

SOUTH PETHERTON In the centre of this view at the depot of Hutchings & Cornelius in South Petherton, Somerset, on 5 August is RYA 700L, an ECW-bodied Bristol VRT new to H&C in 1973. In June 1979 it was sold to a dealer, then was acquired by West Wales of Tycroes in August 1979. By August 1983 it was with a dealer and was sold to Stevenson's of Spath for spares, being eventually scrapped by October 1985. On either side of the VRT are WYD 306H and WYD 928H, Willowbrook-bodied AEC Reliances new in November 1969; the former passed to Safeway on the closure of H&C in May 1979 and remained in that fleet until 1981, while WYD 928H was acquired by Brutonian at the same time and remained there until disposal in October 1987. *Bob Gell*

Photo	DESTINATIONS
77	DOVER
78	LONDON
79	LONDON
80	LONDON
81	LONDON
82	LONDON
83	KINGSTON-ON-THAMES
84	KINGSTON-ON-THAMES
85	KINGSTON-ON-THAMES
86	SWANSEA
87	SWANSEA
88	SWANSEA
89	SWANSEA
90	SWANSEA
91	SWANSEA
92	SWANSEA
93	SWANSEA
94	SWANSEA
95	SWANSEA
96	CARDIFF
97	CARDIFF
98	CARDIFF

SOUTH PETHERTON At the Safeway Service depot, on 5 August, is TYD 888 (left), a Duple-bodied AEC Reliance new to Wake's of Sparkford in May 1955 and acquired by Safeway in May 1974, where it remained until 1979 when it was sold into preservation. In the centre is SOR 117, a Duple-bodied Bedford SB3 that Safeway acquired with the business of Ernest Giles (Venture Coaches) of South Petherton in 1964; Safeway sold it to Millman of Buckfastleigh in 1980. On the right is 200 APB, a Burlingham-bodied AEC Reliance new to Safeguard of Guildford in 1956 and acquired by Safeway in 1962; this bus also passed into preservation in 1982. *Bob Gell*

WEYMOUTH In the town's bus station on 1 July is National Travel (Wessex) No 461 (KCK 977H), a Plaxton-bodied Leyland PSU4A/4R new to Ribble in March 1970. *Author's collection*

On this day Virginia Wade won the Wimbledon Women's Singles title in the Queen's Silver Jubilee year and the centenary year of the tournament. It was Wade's first and only Wimbledon title, and her third and final grand slam title overall; she remains the last British woman to win the singles title at Wimbledon.

PORTSMOUTH During 1967 Portsmouth Corporation took delivery of 26 Leyland Panther Cubs, numbered 150 to 175 (GTP 150E to 163E, GTP 164F to 171F, GTP 172E, and GTP 173F to 175F). The first 12 were bodied by Marshall, and the remainder by MCW. Seen on 16 March is No 172 (GTP 172E) with MCW bodywork. *Bob Gell*

On this day I bought three albums from the Top 30 album charts: Fleetwood Mac's Rumours, *David Bowie's* Low *and the Eagles'* Hotel California.

PORTSMOUTH The next buses purchased new by Portsmouth would arrive during 1969, numbered 176 to 187 (NTP 176H to 187H). Marshall-bodied AEC Swifts, all 12 would be withdrawn in 1981. Working route 6 to Cosham at The Hard on 16 March is No 181 (NTP 181H). *Greg Booth*

PORTSMOUTH The first ECW Bristol VRTs new to Southdown were OCD 763G to 772G, which arrived between March and April 1969; they had been ordered by Brighton Hove & District prior to acquisition by Southdown. Representing this batch en route to Southsea on 16 March is OCD 767G. *Bob Gell*

PORTSMOUTH Working a limited-stop service to Southsea on the same day is Hants & Dorset No 3346 (NEL 120P, an ECW-bodied Bristol VRT new to the company in July 1976. It remained with Hants & Dorset and Hampshire Bus Company until its sale to Magic Bus/Stagecoach in September 1989. In April 1994 it was sold to Enterprise and Silver Dawn, where it remained until June 1996. Sold for scrap, it was painted in London Transport red and exported to Spain by May 1998. *Greg Booth*

SOUTHSEA In National white coach livery on 16 March is Southdown No 1231 (LCD 231F), a Plaxton Panorama-bodied Leyland PSU3 new in 1968. I remember this type of coach working the day service south from the North West to Portsmouth and Southsea, one of the through joint Yelloway/ Associated Motorways services from the North West to the South Coast established for the summer 1967 season. A working initially covered by Royal Blue, after the first or second season it was assigned to Southdown. *Greg Booth*

Below: **FAREHAM** At the town's bus station, also on 16 March and about to take on passengers for the local service to Fareham, is Hants & Dorset No 1629 (RLJ 348H). This bus, when new in 1970, featured four-piece jack-knife doors, a revised entrance layout with deeper steps, and a less ramped gangway. Emerging from the depot in the background is an ECW-bodied Bristol FS, new to Hants & Dorset in 1960. *Greg Booth*

Above: **MAIDSTONE** During 1975 Nottingham purchased 16 Duple-bodied Leyland PSU3B/4Rs, numbered 13 to 28, then between November 1976 and February 1977 14 of the batch were acquired by Maidstone Borough Council. Second from the right in this view taken on 27 March at Maidstone Armstrong Way depot is GRC 883N, with HNU 121N alongside, both having just arrived and still in the Nottingham lilac livery. *Bob Gell*

On this day at Tenerife in the Canary Islands in a collision between a KLM 747 and a PanAm 747, 583 people lost their lives, the deadliest accident in aviation history.

Below: **DOVER** In the depot on 4 February is East Kent GJG 737D, a Park Royal-bodied AEC Regent V new in December 1965. Note the yellow 'Pay on Entry' sign; all 30 of these buses, new between December 1965 and April 1966, were converted for one-person operation, this vehicle being converted in October 1971. The Park Royal-bodied AEC Reliance to the right, WFN 512, was sold for scrap five months after this view was taken. *Author's collection*

On this day Fleetwood Mac's Rumours album was released in the USA.

Above: **DOVER** East Kent turned to Alexander for its final batch of AEC Swifts, YJG 581K to 592K, which were delivered between November and December 1971. They were confined mainly to Dover town services, but later in their lives appeared on longer-distance routes as AEC Reliances were withdrawn. Unlike some Swifts elsewhere, the East Kent examples, with their 11.3-litre AH691 engines, lacked neither speed nor power and were well suited to the hilly terrain around Dover and the high speeds of some East Kent rural routes. Working a Dover local service on 18 April is YJG 588K. *Author's collection*

On this day the Embassy World Snooker Championships moved to the Sheffield Crucible and attracted television coverage for the first time.

DOVER Working the frequent main-road route to Folkestone from Dover on 15 May is YJG 592K, another of the Alexander-bodied AEC Swifts new in December 1971. *Author's collection*

On this day Liverpool FC were English League Champions for the tenth time.

LONDON All the photographs in this section were taken on 4 August. A small batch of nine UTIC U2043 integrals manufactured in Portugal were imported into the UK by Loughborough dealer Moseley's. The first was registered in August 1971 and was purchased by L. F. Bowen of Birmingham. Bowen's only kept it for two months, but then surprisingly purchased two others in 1974, which had previously been operated by Bonas of Coventry. Also in 1974 Charles Cook of Biggleswade purchased a new UTIC U2043, RBM 426M, with Moseley Continental bodywork. These coaches used AEC running gear, and this vehicle had an AEC Swift engine and ZF gearbox. It is seen here in Constitution Hill in the distinctive fleet livery; it was sold in 1980 to Brown of Warboys. *Bob Gell*

LONDON In Central London we see United Counties No 269 (KRP 269E), an ECW-bodied Bristol RELH6G new in April 1967; it had received the National Bus Company white livery in May 1973. *Bob Gell*

The excellent Ted Nugent was in concert at Hammersmith Odeon just a few days after this view was taken.

LONDON No RM1899 (ALD 899B) entered service in May 1964 on route 15 from Upton Park depot. In September 1967 it was repainted at Aldenham Works and transferred to Tottenham depot, where it stayed for the remainder of its service life, being sold for scrap in August 1985. In February 1977 it was repainted in Silver Jubilee livery, sponsored by Avia, and carried a new fleet number, SRM20. It entered service on 11 April together with 24 other Routemasters, and is seen in Victoria. During November of that year the bus was repainted in red and reverted to its original fleet number. *Bob Gell*

LONDON The Leyland Titan B15 prototype, NHG 732P, the forerunner of the Leyland Titan, was built at Park Royal with Leyland parts. It was initially operated by London Buses from November 1975 out of Chalk Farm depot on routes 3 and 24, and this view shows it working service 24 at Victoria. During 1978 it returned to Leyland, and much later, in 1989, was acquired by K. & M. Gagg of Bunny in Nottinghamshire. *Bob Gell*

LONDON Ribble caused something of a sensation at the start of the motorway era by introducing the 'Gay Hostess' double-deck coaches. Having covered many miles they were replaced in 1970/71 by a new design of ECW-bodied VRL coaches, following on from a prototype built in 1968. These were unusual in having longitudinal engines rather than transverse, Ribble choosing the Leyland 0.680 Power Plus engine for this application. Although very impressive-looking vehicles, they developed a reputation for unreliability and were supplanted on long -distance work by Leyland Leopard coaches. In total 30 were acquired and all were in the Standerwick fleet until 1974, when coaching operations were transferred to National Travel Northwest. In Victoria we see LRN 58J, an ECW-bodied Bristol VRLL in the fleet of Destination London; this coach had been new to Ribble in 1971 and passed to National Travel (North West) in April 1974. In August 1976 it was acquired by Ensign Travel and two months later was purchased by Destination London. *Bob Gell*

KINGSTON-ON-THAMES London Country No RMC1496 (496 CLT) is a Park Royal-bodied AEC Routemaster new in 1962, and remained with London Country until 1979. *Bob Gell*

Studio 7 is showing The People That Time Forgot, *sequel to* The Land That Time Forgot, *which had been released in August 1975. Both featured actor Doug McClure, perhaps best known for his role as Trampas in* The Virginian, *which ran on TV from 1962 to 1971.*

KINGSTON-ON-THAMES In the town's bus station, working service 219 to Weybridge, is No RF428 (MXX 405), an AEC Regal IV that entered service from West Green depot in February 1953. By June 1977 it was stationed at Kingston depot, where it worked on services 218 and 219. On 30 March 1979 it was one of the last RFs to be withdrawn from service, and was sold for scrap in December of that year. At this time London Transport still had a number of RF-operated routes that were unsuitable for Leyland Nationals – even the short LSs – due to width restrictions. In the case of Kingston garage, the centre of RF operations in Surrey, the restriction was the width of the inspection pits! Despite the Aldenham renewal programme, the RFs were getting old, passing their quarter-century of intensive town service. The Bristol LH was chosen as a replacement, probably because it was the only narrow bus still made!

On the right is No BL8 (KJD 408P), which entered service on the 216 route from Kingston in September 1976, remaining there until October 1981 when it was stored in Aldenham and subsequently sold for scrap in March 1982 after less than six years of service. *Bob Gell*

KINGSTON-ON-THAMES After a trial with six Leyland Nationals, Nos LS1 to LS6, in November 1973, London Transport purchased 51 of them between May and September 1976, which were a cancelled order from Venezuela. All 51, together with Nos LS1 to LS6, were allocated to Hounslow depot where they worked services 81, 82, 116 and 203, as illustrated in this view of four of them, two of which can be identified, Nos LS26 and LS34 (KJD 526P and KJD 534P). No LS26 would remain at Hounslow until June 1983 when it was transferred to Bromley until sold for scrap in December 1989. No LS34 would remain at Hounslow until March 1984, and was then transferred to Harrow Weald in September 1984, being sold for scrap in March 1991. *Bob Gell*

SWANSEA The photographs in Swansea were all taken on 18 March. In the first, working service 28 to Tycoch, is South Wales No 815 (CCY 985C), a Willowbrook-bodied AEC Regent V new in 1965; I think the Willowbrook bodywork of this style suited the Regent V and made for an attractive bus. Out of the batch of 21 AEC Regent Vs new in 1965, 11 had been withdrawn by the end of 1977. *Bob Gell*

Two weeks earlier AC/DC had appeared at the Top Rank in Swansea.

SWANSEA In this comparison of old and new, and a difference in bodywork height, on the left is South Wales No 824 (CCY 994C), a Willowbrook-bodied AEC Regent V new in 1965. On the right No 905 (OCY 905R) is an ECW-bodied Bristol VRT/SL3/501 new in late 1976. Note that 905 is indicating to turn right but is in the wrong lane to do this manoeuvre. *Bob Gell*

Above left: **SWANSEA** The United Welsh fleet was acquired by South Wales on 1 January 1971 and was at the time of purchase completely made up of Bristol vehicles. This is No 620 (SCY 463G), an ECW-bodied Bristol RELL6G new to United Welsh in 1969. *Bob Gell*

The No 1 single from 12 March was Chanson D'Amour *by Manhattan Transfer.*

Above right: **SWANSEA** Nearest the camera is No 832 (GWN 860D), a Willowbrook-bodied AEC Regent V new in 1966. Following it is No 844 (GWN 872E), new in 1967. The last route to be operated by the AEC Regent Vs was the 14, and this was because of a tight corner, which required short buses, at the Plough & Harrow public house at Murton. The Regent Vs were therefore replaced by one-person-operated (OPO) Bedford YMQs on 7 February 1982, and the remaining AEC Regent Vs continued in service until the 27th of that month. *Greg Booth*

Right: **SWANSEA** This is South Wales No 751 (GCY 751N), a Leyland National new in 1974. *Bob Gell*

Top left: **SWANSEA** During 1967 United Welsh took delivery of two ECW-bodied Bristol RELH6Gs, KCY 211E and KCY 212E. Acquired by South Wales on 1 January 1971 and wearing National Travel white livery with no destination displayed is No 165 (KCY 211E). *Bob Gell*

Centre left: **SWANSEA** Working route 9 to Derwen Fawr is No 441 (NCY 293G), one of 15 Willowbrook-bodied AEC Reliances new to South Wales in 1968. *Bob Gell*

Bottom left: **SWANSEA** Edinburgh Corporation's No 736 (NSF 736), an MCCW-bodied Leyland PD2/20, was new in September 1956 and was transferred to Lothian Region Transport on 16 May 1975. It was then acquired by D Coaches of Morriston in early 1977, and in this view still wears the madder and white livery of Edinburgh Corporation. No 736 would be with D Coaches until withdrawal from service in August 1979. *Bob Gell*

Top right: **SWANSEA** This is No 235 (PWN 235M), one of a large batch Willowbrook-bodied Ford R1014 lightweight buses bought in bulk by National for some of its less fortunate subsidiaries. *Bob Gell*

Right: **SWANSEA** Morris Bros of Swansea ran a contract service between Swansea railway station and the DVLC Offices using a varied selection of buses. This is former Southdown XUF 851, a Northern Counties-bodied Leyland PD3/4 new in 1959. *Bob Gell*

CARDIFF Located adjacent to Cardiff Central railway station, the city's bus station was opened in 1954 and eventually had 34 stands, making it the largest in Wales. During 1976 Merthyr took delivery of five Willowbrook-bodied Leyland PSU3C/2Rs, Nos 203 to 207 (NTX 360R to 364R). In the bus station on 20 November is No 207 (NTX 364R) wearing the orange and white livery that was introduced from 1975. *Greg Booth*

Abba's The Name of the Game *was the No 1 single on this day.*

CARDIFF To accelerate the conversion to one-person operation, numerous vehicles were loaned to Cardiff in late 1977, and one of them was Tyne & Wear PTE No 189 (ETN 89C), a Weymann-bodied Leyland PDR1/1 new in May 1965 and seen here at Cardiff bus station on 20 November. No 189 was on loan from September 1977, then acquired by Cardiff in January 1978, remaining in the fleet until January 1980. *Greg Booth*

Index of Locations and Operators

CARDIFF Also on loan to Cardiff and seen at the bus station on the same day is Bournemouth No 223 (ORU 223G), an Alexander-bodied Leyland PDR1A/1 new in April 1969. *Greg Booth*

The No 1 album on this day was Never Mind the Bollocks, Here's The Sex Pistols, *the only studio album by the English punk rock band. This controversial album is often considered one of the greatest albums of all time and one of the best punk albums, but I was not particularly keen on it.*